Mystery on Heron Shoals Island

Formerly The Curious Affair at Heron Shoals

Written by Augusta Huiell Seaman

Original copyright 1940
Cover design by Phillip Colhouer
Cover illustration by Tanya Glebova
This unabridged version has updated grammar and spelling.
© 2021 Jenny Phillips
goodandbeautiful.com

TABLE OF CONTENTS

I.	Introducing Methuselah	1
II.	Marty Meets the Musical Prodigy	11
III.	The Unwelcome Kilroys	24
IV.	A Clue from the Record	33
V.	Monsieur Has a Theory	43
VI.	One Memorable Day	52
VII.	Footprints in the Sand	61
VIII.	Revelations by Mrs. Greene	70
IX.	Intruder in the Night	80
X.	Morning Adventure	88
XI.	The Hurricane Strikes	99
XII.	On the Trail of Chips	106
XIII.	Hurricane's Harvest	114
XIV.	After the Storm	120
XV.	Aftermath	127
XVI.	Thusy Takes the Spotlight	134
XVII.	Chips Solved the Riddle	142
XVIII.	One November Night	157
	Vocabulary	162

I

INTRODUCING METHUSELAH

THE BIG, DIM KITCHEN WAS very warm and smelled of hot biscuits and baking gingerbread. The late September afternoon sun slanted through a west window, intensifying the velvety green of the tall cedars outside. Within the kitchen it caused the red-checked tablecloth to glow with a burning brilliance. Little old Mrs. Greene bustled about the room, opening and shutting the oven door and putting a shovel or two of coal in the range. Suddenly the rays of sunlight were gone from the west window. The swift, late September twilight had begun. It left the old kitchen dimmer than ever.

"I wonder where Marty can be?" Mrs. Greene muttered aloud, glancing uneasily at the loud-ticking wooden clock on the mantel. (She often thought aloud when she was quite by herself.) "It's half past five now—and the school bus came down at four. She should've been in long ago. I s'pose she's over to the station, as usual, though I told her—"

"Just a minute!—Just a minute!—Just a—" squawked a great blue parrot with a brilliant yellow breast, shuffling about on his high T-perch in a warm corner near the range.

"Oh, hush!" exclaimed Mrs. Greene irritably. "You've been squawking all afternoon, Methuselah. You've got on my nerves!"

"Don't get excited!—Don't get excited!—Don't get—" shrieked the bird, as his mistress lit a big oil lamp and placed it on the table near the window. At that moment the kitchen door burst open, and a bronze-haired girl of fifteen rushed in. Her great brown eyes were sparkling with excitement.

"Nana!" she cried. "What in the world is going on over at the station?" Mrs. Greene surveyed her granddaughter with a slightly inscrutable look but merely replied:

"So that's where you've been this past hour or so! I thought as much! When you've been away from home overnight, like you was last night to play in some silly basketball contest, you know I worry about you till you get home."

"Well, good gracious, Nana!" replied her granddaughter, Marty Greene. "You knew I was staying with Aunt Martha and couldn't possibly come to any harm. Aunt Martha and Uncle Dick came to see the game, and I went home with them right afterward. And we beat the Draketown team to a frazzle!" she ended proudly, then added, "But what's going on over at the station?"

"Why should anything be going on?" countered Mrs. Greene. "It's all closed up by the government and empty now, ain't it? So why should anything be going on? You've been over to your uncle Cy's house—I know that. How are they today? I haven't had time to go over."

"They're all right," declared Marty impatiently. "But something strange is going on. I haven't told you what I saw coming home—after I left the bus where it stops and started to walk home. That's what's got us all guessing!"

"Well, my patience—what did you see!" cried Mrs. Greene, herself now roused to some curiosity.

Marty sat down at the table after throwing aside her beret and sweater. She found some secret satisfaction in keeping her grandmother on tenterhooks, when she could, because Mrs. Greene was of a singularly secretive nature and continually kept Marty in a state of guessing and conjecture. In all other ways, Marty found her grandmother loving, devoted, and self-sacrificing to a degree. Therefore, she sniffed the air now and remarked:

"Ah-h! I smell fresh gingerbread. Give me a slice, Nana, before supper, and then I'll tell you all about it. I'm starving!" Mrs. Greene, who could refuse her most beloved granddaughter nothing, sniffed in pretended indignation, but nevertheless drew a pan of hot gingerbread from the oven and cut Marty a generous slice. The girl ecstatically sank her white, even teeth into it. At that moment the parrot, who had, since Marty's entrance, been quietly resting on his perch, suddenly came to life and squawked:

"Thusy wants a cracker!—Thusy wants a cracker!—Thusy wants—" Marty chuckled and held a bit of gingerbread out to him.

"Don't you give him that, Marty!" commanded Mrs. Greene. "You know as well as I do, it'll make him sick."

"Oh, just a mite, Nana!" begged Marty. "It won't hurt him just once." Methuselah was hopping up and down on his perch in great excitement, but Mrs. Greene sternly answered:

"No! He's been sick before from you feeding him such things—and I have to nurse him through it. I'll give him a soda biscuit and stop his noise." She handed him one from a tin. He took it in his claw, bit into it suspiciously, and threw it contemptuously on the floor of his perch. Then he began the uproar afresh.

"Sometimes he makes me so mad!" sighed Mrs. Greene. "But, tell me now, what was so strange going on over at the station?" Before Marty answered, she finished her gingerbread and waited for the parrot to stop his racket, against which it was impossible to talk. Methuselah, perceiving that no one was paying him any attention, hopped down to the floor of his perch and retrieved his cracker. After that the kitchen grew quiet. When the last crumb of her gingerbread had disappeared, and Mrs. Greene was almost frantic with hidden curiosity, Marty began.

"Funniest thing you ever heard of, Nana. I was walking down the road from where the bus stops at the end of the concrete, and about halfway here there was a great, enormous van, right in the road, and dug in so deep in the sand that it simply couldn't move. You know how terrible our road is from the end of the concrete on to here. Nothing but two sand ruts, and even an ordinary car has trouble getting through it, most times. Well, that van was stuck—and stuck good and proper! I couldn't think why it ever tried it, anyway. There were three men on it, and they were trying their hardest to get out. One was at the wheel, and the other two were pushing at the back, and the wheels were digging in deeper every minute!

"I couldn't get by at all except by going around through the bushes, and when I had, I asked one of the men where the van was goin'. He said 'to the Heron Shoals Coast Guard Station,' and I asked whatever for, as it had been closed up by the government a couple of months ago and all the coast guards had gone. He said he didn't know about that, but those were their orders, and how far away was it? I told him it was about half a mile farther on—same kind of road—and advised them to get some old boards or logs to put under the front tires and that would help them get out of the mess they were in. I told them they could probably find plenty over on the beach just across the dunes, and they started out to hunt for some. But before they left, I asked them what they were bringing down to the station in that big van, and, Nana, what do you think they said?—Two grand pianos!—Did you ever hear of such an absurd thing?"

Mrs. Greene only grunted in reply, but her eyes were veiled in an inscrutable look that was not lost on Marty, who went on:

"They said they'd had orders from the big department store up the coast, where they came from, to bring them down and set them up in the station. That former Captain Greene—that's Uncle Cy—who lived close by, had been informed about it and would see that they were received. That's all they knew about it, and they left me while they walked over the dunes to get some boards.

"I didn't waste a minute after that but hustled down to Uncle

Cy's to hear all about it. Only Gwen was there—and Aunt Emmeline, of course—and they said Uncle Cy was over at the station doing something or other—they didn't know what. Gwen had tried to go out and scout around to find out—she's the most curious little rascal! But Uncle Cy had shooed her back into the house and told her to stay there. So, they didn't know anything about what I'd seen, but you'd better believe they were just about wild when I told them! Gwen was all for flying up the road to see the van, but Aunt Emmeline asked all sorts of questions, too, but I just couldn't make her understand—she's so deaf!

"I knew I ought to come right home, but I just couldn't budge till I'd seen that van get down here—and after a long time, it did. They got it up as near as they could to the station through the sand, and then they opened it and began to unload the pianos. But I'd never have known they were pianos—grand or otherwise—if I hadn't heard it before! They were just two great humpy things all covered with blankets and then a lot of legs, all separate, and a couple of benches. Uncle Cy was superintending getting them in, and when they were all in—and the doors closed—and there wasn't any more excitement, I knew I'd better come on home, so I did. But what do you suppose it's all about?"

Mrs. Greene fussed about the stove a bit with the supper that was cooking before she answered, with her back turned to Marty, "Mebbe they're just going to store them there."

Marty snorted impatiently. "That's impossible, Nana! If they were storing them, they wouldn't take all the wrappings off and set them up, side by side, in the big messroom. And that's just what they were doing. I peeked in the windows when I came away and saw it. No, unless someone's coming down to play on them—or give a concert—I can't imagine what they're for. And, Nana," she ended accusingly, "I do believe you know all about it and won't tell—you act as if you had a secret!"

Mrs. Greene, still stirring things on the stove, shrugged her shoulders, as if giving up the battle, and remarked, "Well, mebbe I do—but I got to get supper on the table, and you'd best go out and fetch in another scuttle of coal. We'll need it. While we're eating, I'll tell you what I know—but not before!"

Marty seized the empty scuttle and, sighing impatiently, went outside to the coal-and-woodshed to fill it up. A purple-colored afterglow still lit the sky in the west, and the air was sweet with the scent of cedars and the pungent odor of fallen leaves. Marty stood still a moment to sniff the air, but the beauty of the outdoors did not afford her the usual keen pleasure, for her mind was disturbed by the foreboding that something unwelcome was coming when her grandmother should disclose what this curious affair was all about. That it was something that might affect their own peaceful daily lives, Marty was pretty well convinced. She shoveled the scuttle full of coal and returned to the house to wait with what patience she could muster till Mrs. Greene had decided to reveal the secret.

Presently they sat down to their simple but appetizing supper of clam chowder, creamed oysters, hot biscuits, and gingerbread, and while they were eating, Marty demanded:

"Now, Nana, go ahead with your story. You promised to tell me while we were having supper. What's been happening while I was away?"

Mrs. Greene took a sip of her tea and remarked, "Well, I don't suppose you're going to like it, but it was something I couldn't very well let go by. You know Professor Sedgwick who always comes here and stays with us while he's doing that surf fishing in the summer and fall. He broke a leg this summer and couldn't get down at all—can't till next year, he wrote—and I missed him a lot. Missed the money he always paid us, too. It went a good way toward helping with the winter."

"I missed him, too," added Marty. "He's such a nice man, so jolly and kind, and no trouble at all about the place. But what about him?"

"Only this about him," went on Mrs. Greene. "About a week ago, he wrote to ask me would I be willing to take in a friend of his for about six weeks, beginning tomorrow. He said this man was very much interested in surf fishing, too, and would like to try it down here. But the main reason was about this man's son—a boy of twelve, I think he said. The boy has been rather ailing lately—not real sick, but just not up to the mark—and he thought it would do the little feller good to be down here for a while. So he wants to bring him, too. And the boy has a sort of teacher that goes around with him, a man, and he's to come along, too. That'll be three of 'em, but Professor Sedgwick wrote that the boy's father was a wealthy man and would be willing to pay anything in reason I'd charge. It was too good a chance to miss, so I didn't feel I ought to refuse. It'll set us up for a good winter, and we won't have to scrimp too much. Now you know!"

Marty put down her fork and groaned. This was worse than anything she had imagined.

"Nana!" she cried despairingly. "How ever are we going to manage it all? This will mean an awful lot of work, and you aren't any too strong, and I have to be away at high school most of the day and ought to study when I get home. I'll have to stay home entirely if you're going to do this—and then I probably won't be able to pass my examinations—and I can't graduate next year!" She pushed her plate away from her and got up to ease her annoyance by striding about the room. At the same moment, the parrot awoke from a nap on his perch and began to shriek, "Don't get excited!—Don't get excited!—Don't—"

"Oh, hush, Methuselah!" cried Marty in complete exasperation.

But Mrs. Greene intervened. "Now you just come and set down, Marty—and listen to me! You ain't heard it all yet. No need to go off like a firecracker that way!" Marty rather sulkily resumed her seat, and Mrs. Greene went on:

"This ain't going to interfere with you at all. I'm going to get enough from it so I can hire Hettie Boscom uptown to come in by the day and do all the heavy work—and you won't have to raise a finger—more'n you do now. And I'll still make a good profit besides. So just calm down! After all, it's only for six weeks." At this news Marty's expressive face cleared, and she began to take more interest in the event.

"Well, maybe it won't be so bad," she conceded, "only I do hate so many strange people about the house and—" A sudden thought occurred to her, and she demanded, "But what's all this got to do with those two grand pianos over at the station?"

Old Mrs. Greene's serious face relaxed, and she almost chuckled as she replied, "Funny thing about that, too! The professor tells me this here little boy, he's a regular musical wonder! Plays so beautiful it's just like a grown person. The teacher that's coming with them—he's a music teacher—and he's training this boy for a big concert he's going to play in this winter. That's what them two pianos are for—so that they can both practice on 'em at once. Funniest idea; I can't see why one wouldn't do."

"But why are they over there at the station?" again demanded Marty, and added, "I suppose there wouldn't be room for them both here."

"That's it, I guess," acknowledged her grandmother. "Seems this boy's father knows the commander of the coast guards very well, and they got permission from Washington to let him use the place this way for the six weeks. I ~~think~~ the practicing'll be done over there! I could never abide banging away on pianos in this house all day!"

They rose to clear away the dishes and wash them at the sink. And when this was over, they both sat down at the table again, which was cleared except for the big kerosene lamp. Marty got out her school books for study, and Mrs. Greene had before her a large, fat, and ~~gaily~~ decorated mail-order catalog that she proceeded to thumb over.

"I've got to order me some more dish toweling and pillow slips," she murmured apologetically. But Marty knew that, incidentally, she was also slyly gloating over the provocative illustration of an elaborate oil burner stove, whose picture in the catalog resembled an overgrown radio cabinet. Her grandmother had had her heart set on a heater like this for several years but had never been able to afford one. It would make all the difference in the world during the winters in this big, chilly old house.

"Maybe she'll be able to afford one now," thought Marty as she wrestled with her algebra. "If she gets enough money for that, I oughtn't to mind all the bother this business is going to be!"

There was little more said between them that evening. Marty had a very heavy schedule of schoolwork to finish, and the old clock on the mantel was striking nine when she finally put her books away, yawned, stretched, and announced that she thought she'd better go to bed early, as she'd been out late the night before. Mrs. Greene was already nodding, half asleep over her catalog. Marty went over to tease the equally sleepy parrot a bit before departing upstairs.

"Wake up, Thusy!" she laughed, poking at his gaudy plumage. He tried to nip her finger and screeched crossly:

"Go away!—Go away!—I'll never tell!—I'll never tell!—I'll—"

"Where'd he ever get that expression, Nana? 'I'll never tell.' He doesn't say it much, but it always makes me wonder who taught it to him." Mrs. Greene's back was turned. She was busy banking the kitchen fire for the night.

"I dunno!" she said. "You better hurry on up to bed."

Marty kissed her goodnight, but as she ascended to her room above, she thought, "Nana certainly does act odd about that parrot, sometimes! I wonder what the secret is about him!"

Snuggling down, later, between the rather chilly sheets, she found it impossible to drop off to sleep at once, as was her usual custom. The excitement and upset of the evening's revelations kept her eyes wide open and her thoughts racing wildly, about the strangers that were soon to invade her peaceful home and all that their sojourn might involve. "I'm certain I'm going to dislike that boy!" she mused resentfully. "Little musical prodigies are always pretty awful, I guess—think the whole world revolves around them! I expect this one's father and teacher'll just sit around adoring him all the time. Well, it'll be interesting to watch, anyhow. What a strange six weeks it's going to be!"

But she little dreamed, as she sank at last to sleep, what an exceedingly curious adventure those six weeks were about to introduce!

II

MARTY MEETS THE MUSICAL PRODIGY

MARTY LEFT THE SCHOOL BUS the next afternoon and fairly raced home along the sandy road that led to the Coast Guard station. Her home was at a considerable distance from her school, which was in a large town across the bay. There was a long bridge across the bay, connecting the little, eight-mile-long Heron Shoals Island with the mainland. On the northern end of this otherwise uninhabited island, there had sprung up, within comparatively recent years, the little town of summer cottages called Surf Crest. But beyond the southern limits of this town, the concrete road ended abruptly, and below it stretched only the rolling dunes and beach on the east of the narrow strip, and on the west, the thickly wooded growths of cedar, holly, and pines. Except for the town, two Coast Guard stations, the home of Captain Cy, and Marty's own abode constituted almost the only other human habitations on the entire island.

As the school bus did not go below the limits of the town, Marty had about a mile of almost impossible road to negotiate before she reached her own home. She had been very inattentive at school all day, her mind absorbed with the new conditions that were about to take place in her home.

"I'm going to dislike him!" she told herself fiercely as she hurried along. "He'll probably be a little, stuck-up child!" She had met that sort in her school, children who could do something special—sing or play the piano, always thinking too well of themselves, always coddled and made much of, generally "teacher's pet." This one was so much more talented that he'd probably be even worse. "How are we going to stand it—six weeks of it?" she asked herself in despair.

Presently she neared the Coast Guard station and hesitated. Should she turn to the right and go straight home through the lane, high-walled with cedars and tall huckleberry bushes, or stop in first at her uncle Cy's house? Now that it came to the point, she really dreaded going straight to the house to meet these strangers. Suddenly, strange sounds from the big white old station, and the sight of Gwen with her face pressed close to one of its windows, decided her. She turned to her left and approached her red-haired and freckled little cousin, demanding, "What's going on, Gwen?" Her nine-year-old cousin simply pointed through the window and said, "Look at that, will you!" Marty looked—and almost collapsed with sudden laughter.

A little, elderly man with wavy, bushy white hair that stood up around his head like a halo was rushing back and forth between the two grand pianos that now stood side by side in the center of the big empty messroom, their tops completely off and looking very dismantled. The man had a tuning implement in his hand and was alternately striking notes and chords on one piano, then on the other, then darting back to tighten some strings on one, then on the other, and muttering all the while to himself in some unintelligible language. Every so often he would lay down the tuning implement and run his hands through his already wildly rumpled hair with a curious motion as if he were trying to tear it out or lift himself up by it.

"He's tuning the two pianos," Gwen informed Marty. "He's

having an awful time with them—says they're in terrible condition. He's the boy's music teacher."

"How do you know?" demanded Marty.

"Because I went in and asked him. His name is Mr. O-bear—something like that. He speaks awful poor English—but he's very nice! I stayed in there awhile, watching him, but then he chased me out—said I asked too many questions but that I could look in from outside."

"Where's the boy?" inquired Marty, almost dreading to be told. She suddenly remembered that she didn't even know his name.

"He's out on the beach with his father," answered Gwen indifferently. "Look at O-bear now—he's tearing his hair again!"

But Marty had temporarily lost interest in the curious little man. She wanted to catch a glimpse of the boy, so she turned away and strolled over the dune toward the wide beach. She hoped she could catch sight of him before being seen herself so that she might have a chance to study him. "He'll probably be strutting around," she thought, "acting as if he owned the whole beach!" But when she reached the top of the dune, there was no one in sight except a tall man clad in fishing togs and high rubber boots, casting a long line into the surf. There was not another soul in sight. Thinking the boy might be wandering around back of the dunes somewhere, she ventured farther toward the surf, coming abreast of an old piece of wreckage that had lain there ever since she could remember. Sometimes, steady high west winds covered it so completely with sand that it was all but invisible. Then a huge northeaster would tear the sand away, leaving it revealed in all its stark, wrecked nakedness—a heavy wooden deck on which several rusty iron capstans still stood like sentinels. It was in this condition at the present moment.

As she was skirting one end, she suddenly stopped short in her tracks. A young boy, invisible till that moment, was sitting with his back against one of the capstans, a pad supported on his knees, a pencil in his hand. He had not heard her approach, and in a swift, appraising glance, she was able to take stock of him before herself being seen.

He was a slender-looking boy of twelve or thereabouts. He had a mat of thick, short, curly black hair. The color of his eyes she could not see for the moment, as he had them bent over his work, but she later discovered them to be an intense, deep blue, accentuated by long, dark lashes. But it was his pale, thin face that interested her most, for it was a very beautiful face and its expression was wistful, "sad," as Marty herself called it. So different was his whole appearance from what she had imagined that she experienced a shock of keen surprise. In the instant that she stood motionless and unobserved, she could not make up her mind whether to go forward and greet him or retreat unnoticed back home and wait for his coming there.

But suddenly he seemed to sense her presence and looked up from his work. In another instant he had scrambled to his feet, dropping his pad and pencil. As she involuntarily came toward him, he held out his hand shyly and said:

"How do you do? I guess you're Marty Greene, aren't you? I'm Ted Burnett."

"Why—why—how did you know my name?" stammered Marty, taking his hand. She noticed that his hand, though thin and fragile looking, had a surprisingly muscular grip. His face lit up with a little smile as he answered:

"Professor Sedgwick has told us all about you—and all about the place here. I feel as if I knew you already quite well!"

Marty was rather stunned. This was something quite different from what she had expected. Far from being the self-important young musical "prodigy" she had expected, he was just a shy young boy trying to be polite. Casting about for some suitable reply, her eye lit on the pad and pencil he had dropped, and he followed her questioning glance.

"I was just working out a little counterpoint," he informed her. "I got tired walking on the beach, and Dad thought I'd better sit here and rest, so I thought I'd work on that counterpoint Monsieur gave me to do. But I didn't get much done. I'd rather watch the sea and the gulls and the teeter-snipe."

Marty hadn't the least idea what "counterpoint" was, but she glanced down at the pad and saw that it was lined with rows and rows of musical staves, on which he had been placing notes and chords.

"Who is Monsieur?" she inquired curiously.

"Oh, I thought you knew!" he said quickly. "He's Monsieur Aubert, my music professor. He's up there at the station now, having an awful time with the two pianos. He says the moving them down here put them in terrible condition." Suddenly he changed the subject, commenting shyly, "I like your parrot Methuselah! I've never been near a real, live parrot before—except in the zoo. This one talks so well—and he nearly bit my finger off at lunch time when I tried to give him a cracker. Monsieur tried talking French to him, and Methuselah acted oddly. Didn't squawk at him at all but just sat staring at him as if he were somehow trying to understand! He's an odd bird, isn't he?"

This information rather astonished Marty, who had always sensed that there was something curious about Methuselah and particularly about her grandmother's reluctance to talk about his origin. Odd that this boy should have hit on the same idea almost at once! She was about to reply that Thusy certainly was odd when she happened to glance toward the fisherman off at the edge of the surf. "Look!" she cried. "Your father's just caught a big fish—I think it's a striped bass! Let's go down and look at it!" And they both hurried off to join Mr. Burnett, who had that moment landed his prize—a seven pounder—and was busy disengaging the hook. Looking up, he saw the pair and called out:

"This is Marty, I know. How do you do? I feel as if I knew you very well already from Professor Sedgwick's talks about you." Then he dropped the fish on the sand, wiped his hand on the towel or cloth that all surf-fishermen seemed to have draped on them for that purpose, and held out his hand to Marty.

"Isn't he a beauty?" he cried, pointing to the bass, whose jewel-like sides glittered in the afternoon sun. "Must be more than six pounds if he weighs an ounce—and he certainly gave me a bit of a battle! I promised Mrs. Greene I'd bring her back a fish for supper, but I guess she didn't think I'd have any success, for she said she'd have something else anyway, in case they weren't biting. We can all make a meal out of this fellow!" The remark about her grandmother suddenly recalled to Marty the fact that she was expected back at home directly on her return from school, so she said something to that effect and offered to carry the fish back with her, that it need not get stale lying on the sand.

But Mr. Burnett laughingly replied, "Indeed I shan't burden you with this big fellow! A fisherman proud as I am of his catch always wants to carry it himself. In any case, it's getting late, and the sun is well down, and it's growing a bit chilly. Ted ought to go in, too, so we'll all go back together."

While he reeled in his line and then strung a piece of cord through the big fish's gills, in order to carry it more easily, Marty had a chance to take stock of this newcomer also. She decided that he was a very handsome man, big and stalwart, with a shock of arresting gray hair and clear, penetrating gray eyes. His manner was friendly and wholly natural, and she knew she was going to like him. And as they trudged back across the wide beach to the station, she was inwardly marveling that, so far, not a word had been said about the talents of the young musical prodigy—no reference at all to his playing. Nor was there the slightest suggestion of "high-hatting anybody" (as she privately called it) or the assuming of any supercilious airs. "Maybe I was mistaken," she thought. "Maybe it isn't going to be like that at all!"

As they were crossing the high dunes by the path a short distance from the station, Professor Aubert came to the door and beckoned and called to Ted to come in for a few moments to try the pianos with him.

MARTY MEETS THE MUSICAL PRODIGY

"Run along, Ted!" said Mr. Burnett. "You can come back later with Monsieur. But don't let him keep you too long. We don't want to keep supper waiting!" The boy left them, and Marty and Mr. Burnett pursued their way together. As they approached the long, winding lane that led to the old house, Mr. Burnett, who had been chatting with Marty about her school activities, suddenly switched the subject and began, "Now that Ted isn't with us and we can be alone for a few moments, I want to have a bit of a talk with you, Marty, about that little fellow."

"Here it comes!" thought Marty. "Now he's going to tell me what a talented child he is!" She quite regretted that thought later.

"You see," went on Mr. Burnett, "I feel that I know you very well, through the many fine things I've heard about you from Professor Sedgwick. And as the circumstances about Ted are worrying me a great deal, I feel as if I could safely confide in your good judgment. Ted is a rather peculiar little fellow. He has a great musical gift, so I'm told—I know very little about music myself—and he has inherited it directly from his mother, who was a very great and successful musician in the years before I married her. She gave up her musical career when she married me, but when she found that her little son had also inherited her gift, she devoted her time to training him in it, beginning almost from the time he could toddle. And since he seemed to be making such marvelous strides, she was planning to have him give a public recital in New York this year, when he would be twelve."

They were midway through the lane, at this point, and Marty suddenly glanced up at his face, for he had stopped talking abruptly, and stood staring up at the tops of the close-crowding, pointed cedars burnished with the descending sun. His fine face had taken on some grim lines, but his voice was as steady as ever when he continued:

"But we had a very great loss—Ted and I—something less than a year ago. She was taken from us suddenly—a fatal automobile accident—and life will not be quite the same for either of us, ever again. It has been particularly hard on Ted. He's an extremely sensitive child, and he adored her. After the first shock of it was over, I thought perhaps he would abandon the music, as being too painful a memory, and I planned to put him in a good boys' school. I'll admit that I privately hoped he would forget his music and someday fit himself for a business career, perhaps step into my own place later on, when he was ready for it. But I guess that's not to be. He begged me not to send him away to school, but let him stay at home and go on with his music. His one thought seems to be not only a real love of it, but also a desire to fulfill his mother's ambition for him. He seemed so unhappy about my plan that I finally gave it up and engaged his mother's former teacher, this Professor Aubert, to take up the task of his musical instruction, which he was delighted to do. Ted also has another tutor at home to give him instruction in other studies, for I do not want his general education neglected. But he is very fond of 'Monsieur,' as we all call him, so we brought him along on this little vacation. Also, Monsieur does not want Ted to fall behind with his practicing, as he is to give this recital later in the fall. So that explains the two pianos."

Marty had been very quiet all through this account, but her expressive face showed that she appreciated keenly the sorrow that had come into the lives of these people still almost unknown to her. She could find no words to express it, but Mr. Burnett must have understood, for he went on:

"This has been a long story, Marty, but I had to tell it to you that you might understand fully the situation. The point of the whole matter is this: Ted's health hasn't been too good lately. He never was an athletic boy, as so many are, never very fond of outdoor sports and that sort of thing, but he always had been normally well and strong. Of late months, though, he doesn't sleep well, his appetite has failed, and though he says nothing, we know he is brooding deeply over the loss of his mother. We have tried everything—taken him to new places, tried to give him new experiences—everything—but nothing has worked. It was Professor Sedgwick who finally suggested bringing him down here to try a few weeks of an utterly different kind of life, a life of roughing it on this wild beach, with just enough of his piano practice to keep him from falling back there, but mainly to be out in the wind and the sun and the salt air, and the privilege of having the companionship of yourself and your little cousin over at Captain Cy's. If that doesn't take him out of himself, I don't know what will."

"I'm afraid he won't like the house," ventured Marty. "It's so big—and old—and it hasn't any conveniences, not even a bathtub! We couldn't ever afford to put any in."

"He'll get used to it and come to like it!" prophesied Mr. Burnett. "That's all part of the change. You don't realize how we city dwellers enjoy getting away from that kind of life and being down here on this wild, magnificent beach of yours. We don't miss the lack of city conveniences. It's all part of the fun! But before we leave this conversation, there's one more thing I want to say. My main purpose in this stay here is that Ted may have something to divert his mind from past unhappiness. If you can think of any way you can help about that, any special things that might get his mind running in other channels, I'll be eternally grateful to you—and you won't be sorry you took the trouble. It may not come all at once. You don't know him well enough yet. But if, in your further acquaintance with him, you can discover anything, outside his music, that seems to strike his interest, will you be good enough to encourage him in it?"

"I surely will!" promised Marty earnestly, though how it was to be brought about, she hadn't the faintest idea at that moment.

"Thank you!" said Mr. Burnett simply. "And now I think we had better be getting on to the house. I must clean this fish before I can ask Mrs. Greene to cook it—not a very savory job!"

After Marty had snuggled down in bed that night, her mind too excited with the day's events to allow her to sleep, she began to consider the problem with which Mr. Burnett had faced her. She was not in her own room and not entirely comfortable, which fact also served to keep her awake. At her grandmother's suggestion, she had given up her room to the boy because it was warmer and more comfortable than most of those in the big old house at this season of the year, being directly over the kitchen and getting some of the kitchen's heat through a little register set in the floor. She had rather resented this change up till now—hating to give up her own cozy nook that she had filled with her personal belongings and inexpensive decorations. Now she was glad she had done so, even though the room she was in was not too well furnished and had been long unused.

"After all, what did it matter?" she thought, trying to find a comfortable spot on the hard, lumpy old mattress. She had given her word to try to help this interesting boy, and that was the only thing that counted. What an evening they'd had, all gathered at supper about the kitchen table! Her grandmother hadn't liked that very much, at first. She had begun setting places for the newcomers in the long-unused dining room, trying to heat it as well as she could with a little oil stove, for the evening had turned chilly. But when Mr. Burnett had seen it, he demanded that they all eat together in the cozy, big, old kitchen, said they'd like it and it would be so much less trouble than setting a separate table. Mrs. Greene had agreed somewhat reluctantly, considering that it didn't quite fit in with the proprieties.

Marty had never remembered a more interesting meal. The willing but clattering Hettie Boscom had gone home just before the supper was served, and Marty herself waited on the table when it was necessary. The conversation had been as natural and cheerful as if they had all known each other a long time. Often it was dominated by the lively little old French professor.

"How polite he is!" thought Marty. "He bowed over my hand when he was introduced as if I were a great lady, instead of just Marty Greene! And he insists on calling me '*Mam'selle* Marty'! And how he loves that little boy! He watches every expression of his face—almost every mouthful he eats!"

During the meal, Mr. Burnett had explained how he had come to be allowed to house the two pianos in the Coast Guard

MARTY MEETS THE MUSICAL PRODIGY

station—a most unusual proceeding according to all precedent.

"I had a pretty complicated time about that," he had remarked laughingly. "Had to pull every wire I was able to. Fortunately, I had some acquaintance with the commander in New York, who got me in touch with some of the officials in Washington. As this particular station has been closed and all the crew sent elsewhere, as they have done with a number along this coast, I had thought the matter would be simple. It was anything but that! Official 'red tape' was all against it. I finally had to promise that should the slightest government need for the station arise while the pianos were there, I would move them out at an instant's notice, even if I had to leave them out in the sand!" They had all giggled at the vision of the two stately grand pianos reposing on a sand dune!

And how badly Methuselah had behaved at the beginning of the meal! He had squawked and screeched and demanded a cracker with such an earsplitting racket that Mrs. Greene had finally removed him, perch and all, to the darkness of the dining room, where he immediately became silent. Marty noticed that Ted had been watching him with interested eyes and a distinct smile. But when he was gone, the boy's face fell into its usual serious expression.

There had been one curious little occurrence after the meal was over. When the dishes were removed and Marty was washing them, all the newcomers had insisted on helping to dry and put them away, much to Mrs. Greene's disapproval. But they had made it a rather hilarious occasion, even Ted joining the affair, and were laughing and joking like old comrades before the task was finished. Then, at Ted's request, Marty brought the parrot in once more and let Ted give him his supper of rice and sliced banana. While he was eating it, Mr. Burnett had remarked:

"This parrot interests me very much, Mrs. Greene. And, by the way, he isn't a true parrot. He is of the parrot family, but he is really a macaw. His brilliant blue and yellow plumage is quite different from that of the common green parrot. This type comes from central Brazil and is uncommonly intelligent and usually very long lived. Sometimes they are said to live as long as seventy-five or eighty years. And they have wonderful memories, too, I understand. This Methuselah's name is very appropriate, for I think he is quite an old bird. How long have you had him, Mrs. Greene?"

It had seemed such a simple question—one to which an ordinary answer might have been simply returned. But to the surprise of everyone but Marty, Mrs. Greene's wrinkled countenance had flushed, and she had answered hesitantly and a bit grudgingly, "Oh, about twenty-five years or so, I guess!" And before any further queries could be put, she had hurried out of the kitchen mumbling something to the effect that she must "see to some things upstairs." Mr. Burnett had then turned to Marty herself and remarked, "Your grandmother doesn't seem to care to talk much about Thusy's past, does she! I hope I haven't offended her by asking too many questions."

"Oh, Nana's always been like that about Thusy!" she had replied. "There must be some secret about that bird that she doesn't want to talk about. She won't even talk to me when I've asked questions."

"Well, then, we mustn't annoy her by asking any more of them," Mr. Burnett had said, considerately. Marty noticed that Ted had been listening wide-eyed to this exchange of remarks, but the boy offered no comment and turned to the professor who was standing in front of Thusy, chattering softly to the parrot in French. And Thusy was listening with bright unwinking gaze and head cocked to one side as if the little Frenchman's remarks interested him tremendously.

"Zis bird, he understand zee French, I know he do!" declared the professor, running his hands excitedly through his white hair. "He leesten like he has heard eet before, many, many time, but long ago. Now see! I try to expereement, I try to make heem say somesing after me!"

He placed himself squarely in front of the parrot's perch, looking the bird straight in the eye, and began slowly and distinctly:

"*Bonjour,* Thusy! *Bonjour, bonjour, bonjour!*" The parrot looked at him intently with his bright eyes unwinking, as if trying hard to understand. Then he began a low mumbling, as if to himself, and the sound he made certainly resembled something like "*bum-bum-bum-bum.*" They all listened in a breathless silence till the professor whispered:

"Wait!—I theenk he ees getting eet. He perhaps say somesing!"

And Methuselah did. After a long moment of silence, he suddenly stood erect on his perch, flapped his wings, and screeched at the professor:

"Go fly a kite!" Then he turned his back insultingly, tucked his head under his wing, and prepared to go to sleep for the night.

A peal of laughter from Ted greeted this unexpected reply—the first time Marty had heard him really laugh, and they all joined in, even the discomfited Professor Aubert.

"That was dreadful!" cried Marty. "Somebody must have taught him that. He says it every once in a while—and always where it comes in just right. But it did sound awful—and after all the trouble you took, Professor!" The professor did look rather crestfallen but continued to insist that he was right and would prove it later.

But Mr. Burnett said, "No more of this now! I hear Mrs. Greene coming downstairs." And the subject was dropped for the night.

Marty thought it all over, lying on her lumpy bed, and suddenly an idea popped into her mind. So startling was it that she sat straight up in bed muttering, "The very thing! Why didn't I think of it before? Ted's interested in that parrot, not only because he's an unusual bird but because there's some mystery about him. That settles it! I'm going to get Ted even more interested in Thusy and the mystery, and perhaps we can both solve it together. I always did want to know what it was all about, anyway. And perhaps it'll help Ted to—forget for a while!"

She lay down again in a pleasant sort of contentment and tried to plan how she would go about it. And presently she fell asleep.

III

THE UNWELCOME KILROYS

MARTY AND TED SAT TOGETHER on a high, steep dune overlooking the sea. It was a warm, golden, perfect afternoon—the type of weather that often comes to the coast in the early fall. The sea before them was a vivid floor of green-blue, with only small wavelets lapping in at the water's edge—an ideal day for surf casting. Swooping gulls, silhouetted against the intensely blue sky, gleamed with an unbelievable whiteness. The air was pungent with the odor of salt and pine and cedar, wafted by the light west wind from across the bay.

Marty had just strolled out to the beach after having finished helping Mrs. Greene with some preparations for supper. It being Sunday, Hettie Boscom had gone home directly after the dinner dishes were disposed of. Marty found Ted sitting on the dune watching his father and Monsieur who were both down by the sea's edge, intent on casting long fishing lines far out beyond the overfall. Monsieur had been eager to learn the fine art of surf casting, and Mr. Burnett was engaged in his instruction. Ted was idly watching the performance, his serious little face still bearing its usual, wistful expression. But Marty, as she slipped down beside him, noted that he had lost his pallid color, though he had only been there for two days, and that his nose had a distinctly sunburned tinge. She had also observed that he was beginning to be slightly interested in his meals. Plainly the sun, the sea, and the salt air were beginning their salutary work.

"But he isn't any different in his mind yet!" thought Marty. "If only he could be more really cheerful—and not just politely pretend to be when he isn't! I wish I could find the chance to get him interested in the mystery about Thusy. Maybe this is a good time. We've all been too busy since Friday when they first arrived."

"The professor is doing very well with his casting, isn't he!" she remarked, as Ted looked up to greet her with a slight smile.

"He has strong arms, and I s'pose that must help," said Ted, as they watched Monsieur reel in a long cast and prepare to hurl it out again. But even as they watched—something went wrong! The professor had just swung his rod back over his shoulder and then far forward to give the metal squid on the end of the line momentum enough to carry it far out into the sea, when a sudden tangling up of his line at the tip of the pole caught it—and held it fast. His reel, however, with hundreds of feet of line on it, went right on spinning out of the line, which, having no outlet through the tip of the pole, came billowing around him in yards and yards of hopeless tangle. And in an instant he stood there with a mess of line like a great wuzzey ball in his astonished hands.

Something about the little Frenchman's predicament seemed to strike Ted's sense of humor. For the second time since Marty had known him, he burst into a spontaneous peal of laughter, in which she had to join.

"He's always getting into trouble like that!" chuckled Ted. "And he's always so funny about it. Look at him now!" Monsieur had hurled his pole to the ground in deep chagrin and was running his hands wildly through his hair. And while Mr. Burnett was sympathizing with him, he shouted, "I weel feesh no more zis day! I take heem to zee station and untangle heem zere!" And he grabbed up his pole, with its great wad of matted line, and trotted up the beach toward the station, not even looking at the children on the dune as he went. Mr. Burnett resumed his fishing alone.

"He takes these things so hard!" commented Ted. "Like the other night when Thusy acted so badly with him." Marty murmured that it was too bad if such little things hurt his feelings, but her thoughts were on the opening Ted had just given her in the mention of the parrot. Here was her chance! She could commence talking about him without effort, and she began:

"Speaking of Thusy—has Monsieur made any progress with him in trying to get him to talk French?"

"He's been trying," said Ted. "I heard him yesterday when he thought no one else was around, working hard to get Thusy to say something. I was passing outside the window, coming over to the beach. But I haven't heard how he got on. Thusy's an odd bird, isn't he!"

"He's odder than you think!" agreed Marty eagerly. "Do you know, I've always thought there was some strange mystery about that parrot. He says the oddest things sometimes. I can't imagine where he learned them. And Nana always acts so peculiar about him—as if she knew some secret she wouldn't tell!" Ted's serious little face lit up, and his eyes began to sparkle.

"Oh, tell me what you know—please, Marty! I do so like a mystery!" This was an even more enthusiastic response than she had expected. Now was the time to plunge into it.

"Well," she said, "I hardly know anything at all about the thing, but I'll tell you what I do know—and some of the things I suspect. Thusy's always been here, as long as I can remember—and long before I was here myself. You see, my father and mother are both dead. I lost them when I was a baby. Father was Nana's oldest son. After he died, my mother didn't live very long, and then Nana took me to live with her. Thusy was here when I came, so I've sort of grown up with him. Mostly I never think much about him but sometimes, when he says something odd, he makes me wonder about him. I remember asking Nana, when I was quite young, where she got him. All she'd say was that someone who stayed here long ago had him and gave him to her and she's kept him ever since. And when I asked who it was, she said I asked too many questions and not to bother her about it. And that's all I ever did get out of her. I don't know why she doesn't want to talk about it, but she acts like that about a lot of things. It's her way, I guess!" Ted had been listening to all this with breathless interest.

"But doesn't anyone else know?" he demanded. "How about Captain Cy? He's one of her sons, too, isn't he? He was telling Dad this morning quite a lot about this place. Said he'd been skipper at this station for fifteen years before he retired this last year. Surely he ought to know!"

"I asked him once about it, too," said Marty, "but he said Nana had had Thusy so long he couldn't remember about when she did get him—thought some sailor or coast guard or someone like that had left him with her. You see, he left home when he was quite a young boy and went to sea for a long while. When he left the sea, he came back and became a coast guard himself and was sent to a station way down the coast, so he didn't know much about what went on at home here. I guess he doesn't know any more about Thusy than the rest of us do."

Ted mulled over this in silence for a few minutes. Then he asked, "But you said Thusy says some strange things once in a while. What are they? I haven't heard him say that kind of thing yet."

"Well," replied Marty thoughtfully, "once in a while, without any reason, he suddenly says, 'I'll never tell!' Keeps repeating it over and over. And just once, when Nana wasn't around and I was alone with him in the kitchen, he woke up from a nap and began to shriek—'Hide it, Jack!—Hide it!—I'll never tell!' That was odd, wasn't it? I never dared ask Nana about it."

"My, but that was strange!" commented Ted. "I wonder who Jack was—and what was going to be hidden?"

"If we knew that," said Marty sagely, "we'd know a lot more than we do about the mystery. Maybe 'Jack' was the person who owned him first."

"Do you always keep Thusy chained to his perch?" demanded Ted, veering to another angle of the subject. "Don't you ever let him fly around loose?"

"Nana used to let him fly around the kitchen when she cleaned his perch," said Marty. "She'd close all the windows and doors while he was free, and he liked it a lot. But she won't do it anymore. She makes him get in an old parrot cage she has while she cleans up now."

"Why's that?" questioned Ted.

"Well, about three years ago, an odd thing happened one day," Marty went on. "I was away at school, and Nana locked up the house—shut everything tight—and walked up to town to do some marketing. When she got back, Thusy was gone! He wasn't on his perch and part of the chain was lying on the bottom of it. She saw at once what had happened. The chain was very old and rusty, and Thusy had somehow managed to gnaw through one of the links and get away. She thought, of course, she'd find him around the house somewhere. She was sure he couldn't have gotten out because every door and window was shut. But, though she searched in every nook and corner, and called and called him—there wasn't a sign of him to be found. She thought she'd lost him for good, and she felt so bad about it that I found her crying when I got back from school.

"I said he simply must be in the house, and let's hunt for him again. So we went over the house from top to bottom. We even hunted way up in that lookout tower on the roof, and then we went down to the cellar. But no Thusy! But you'll never guess what we found when we got back to the kitchen at last—there was Thusy sitting on his perch, with a piece of chain dangling from his leg, just as if he'd never been away! And when he saw us, he began to chuckle, just as if he was laughing at us! And we've never discovered to this day where he could have hidden himself!"

"Well, that was the oddest thing!" commented Ted. "He couldn't have been out of the house at all."

"He must have been!" cried Marty. "There wasn't a corner we didn't search—under the beds and other furniture—everywhere! There just wasn't any place he could have hidden. And yet, if he got out of the house, I can't imagine how he did, for there wasn't a window or door open so much as a crack." They pondered in silence for a few moments over the mystery. Presently Ted changed the subject again.

"It's strange about that old house you live in," he commented, glancing back at the upper floors and cupola that were visible from where they sat, rising above the clustering cedars well back of the station. "It's such a big house—almost the only one on this long stretch of beach, except Captain Cy's opposite the station. How did it come to be here?"

"Why, Grandfather Greene—Nana's husband—built it when he was in the Coast Guard station here. They used to live over across the bay, as most coast guardsmen do, but he didn't like the long trip to get back home, so he built this house for them to live in the rest of their lives. He died a long time ago, but Nana has always kept on living here. She likes it and won't ever live anywhere else. I'd much rather live across the bay in town where you could have a nice house and electricity and all that sort of thing, and I'd be near school. But she wouldn't move—and we couldn't afford it anyway—so here we stay!"

"I think it's a lovely place," said Ted. "I'd like to live here all the time. It's so quiet and peaceful—and right by the ocean. Somehow even the music sounds different here from what it does anywhere else!"

As if to verify his last remark, there was wafted through the open windows of the station the sound of some resonant chords and then the opening bars of a Chopin polonaise. Evidently the professor had wearied of the task of untangling his fishing line and was consoling himself with music. The two on the dunes sat silent, listening to the rich chords and rippling runs. They seemed to fit in with the mood of the perfect day, carrying the spirit to heights of ecstasy.

"He plays beautifully!" said Marty softly, when the echo of the last chords had died away. She herself loved music, though she had no talents to produce any.

"Yes, he's a master," acknowledged Ted, and ended wistfully, "I hope someday I'll be able to play like that!"

"I haven't heard you play yet," remarked Marty, "and you've been here nearly three days."

"I'm just having a little holiday," said the boy. "Dad didn't want me to begin real practice till Monday, so that I could get a little used to the place first. I did try the pianos out with Monsieur on Friday, but—"

He got no further, for Marty, who had been looking down the beach as they were talking, suddenly gripped his arm and exclaimed:

"Oh! Look who's coming! Why on earth did they have to land over here just now—and spoil our lovely afternoon?"

"Why, who is it?" demanded Ted, looking in the direction she indicated and seeing only, in the distance, two people, evidently a woman and a young lad of sixteen or seventeen, plodding along through the sand.

"Never mind, I can't explain right now!" muttered Marty. "I don't think they've seen us yet. We'll have a chance to get into the station by that little back door. Hurry, and keep as much out of their sight as possible!"

She sprang up, with Ted following her and wondering very much what it was all about and the reason for this hasty retreat. Skirting around the side of a dune, they managed to slip into the rear door of the station that led into its former kitchen without (so Marty wildly hoped) being seen by the advancing pair. As they stood panting for breath in the dismantled kitchen, Ted demanded:

"Who are they? Why don't you want to see them?"

"Because they're troublemakers!" cried Marty impatiently. "They always have been! They're enemies of Nana's. That's another thing

I don't know what it's all about, for Nana won't tell me. But I think it goes back to some quarrel or other way back in Grandpa's time. This Mrs. Kilroy's father and Grandpa were both coast guards in this station at the same time. And something happened and they had a falling-out. It's all very silly, seems to me, so long ago and both of them dead now! But Mrs. Kilroy has never forgotten it and comes over here and tries to fight it all out with Nana every once in so often. Nana always sends me away so I shan't hear it. But it generally makes her pretty sick afterward. They must have rowed across the bay this afternoon and walked up the beach. Odd thing, too! Thusy seems to be mixed up in that quarrel. I once was out in the garden picking peas when Mrs. Kilroy was here and was just leaving. And she called back to Nana, just as she opened the door, 'And that parrot ought to be ours, by rights, and you know it!' Of course, as I wasn't supposed to hear what they were saying, I couldn't ask Nana about it. It's all very curious!"

Just at this point they glanced out of the little window and saw the pair in question trudging through the sand past the Coast Guard station, on their way to the old house back in the cedars. They were casting curious glances at the station, for the professor was still playing, and they were plainly bewildered at these sounds of melody emerging from so unlikely a source. The young lad made a motion as if to steer his mother up toward the station door to investigate, but she pulled him back peremptorily, and they continued on their way. At the same moment, the music stopped. Monsieur had also seen them through the window and called out to Marty and Ted, whom he had heard talking in the kitchen:

"Who ees zis who goes by zis so unfrequented place?" The two came into the mess hall where the pianos stood, and Marty explained to him the unlooked-for invasion. And Ted supplemented the account by giving him some of the curious facts about Thusy that he had just learned from Marty. Monsieur ran his hands through his hair and wrinkled his brows in solemn thought. Then he broke in, "Ah! Zee parrot! How strange ees zis mystery about heem! But listen, *mes enfants—moi*, I make one deescoveree about heem only yesterday. I talk to heem in zee French—oh, zee very long while! He do not answer, but I keep right on. *Alors*—after long, long time, vat you theenk happen? I keep saying to heem, '*Bonjour, Thusy!*' Over and over I say eet. And zen I wait. And zat parrot, he put hees head to one side, and he look like he theenk hard, and zen he say, '*Bon-bon-bonjour*—Monsieur!'" He stopped impressively and waited for their reaction. Both looked slightly puzzled for a moment, and Ted was first to catch the implication of Thusy's response.

"But that's wonderful!" he cried. "If Thusy had just been repeating what you said, it would have been '*Bonjour*, Thusy!,' wouldn't it? Instead he put in 'Monsieur.' But maybe that's because he's heard us calling you 'Monsieur.'"

"*Non, non!*" cried the professor, running his hands wildly through his much-disheveled hair. "Zat cannot be so. Not enough has he heard you say that to me. Only two—three times. Zat '*Bonjour, Monsieur!*' he learn from someone long ago who teach heem zee French. He say eet so perfect—like learn to say eet long ago!" And he ended impressively:

"*Mes enfants*, leesten to me! Zat bird—he once belong to someone who ees French. He know more French zan zat. And me, I am going to find out how much he know!"

IV

A CLUE FROM THE RECORD

THE WEATHER HAD CHANGED. The balmy warmth of the last two days had vanished, and a cold, woolly fog was drifting in from the sea. Marty shivered unconsciously as she was trudging home from school on Monday afternoon, but her thoughts were not on the weather or her own personal discomfort. They were deeply concerned with the doings of the previous day and the progress that was being made in diverting Ted's mind from his own affairs to the mystery that centered in Methuselah.

"And just to think," she mused, "coming down this very road, only last Friday, I told myself I was going to dislike that boy!" She almost blushed at the remembrance. "It only goes to show how little you can tell about people you've never even seen!"

Then her thoughts reverted to the events of the past Sunday afternoon and its rather laughable sequence concerning the visit to the beach of the objectionable Kilroys. She and Ted had remained at the station talking with Monsieur, and all the while she had been wondering how her grandmother was enduring their visit. But before very long they had observed through the window that the Kilroys were again emerging from the lane and obviously coming toward the beach.

"Quick!" she had cried to the others. "They'll be trying to get in here next; I know them! Let's lock the doors and disappear upstairs till they leave!" Ted and Monsieur had not been slow to catch her meaning. Marty had rushed to lock the front entrance and Ted the kitchen door, and then they had all scampered up the winding stairs to the second floor, on tiptoe. And not a moment too soon, either. For they just disappeared from view when there had come a loud thumping on the main door. Scarcely breathing, the trio upstairs stood immovable, listening to a murmur of voices below. Then they had heard footsteps crunching through the sand around toward the rear, and the kitchen door had been rattled and thumped on. Back had come the footsteps and, from the half-heard conversation, it could be distinguished that the pair were gazing in at the lower windows and commenting on the two pianos in great bewilderment. Then the voices and the footsteps had faded away.

"But don't let us show ourselves yet," Marty had warned. "I know what they're going to do next—go over to Uncle Cy's and see if they can get in there. But Uncle Cy and Aunt Emmeline and Gwen have driven over across the bay to visit Aunt Martha, so the house is all locked up. They certainly won't succeed today!"

Peeking out of one of the second-floor windows in the bunkroom, they saw that it was even as Marty had said. The baffled pair had turned away from the little, gray-shingled house opposite, and a quarter-mile walk they would have to re-cross to the bay where they had doubtless moored their boat.

"I wonder if they'll meet Dad now?" speculated Ted. "He's down there fishing. If they start questioning him, he won't know what it's all about!"

"Maybe he isn't there," Marty had replied. "I noticed he started moving down the beach soon after Monsieur left him, and I think he was going to try out a place about a mile farther down. Nana was telling him today that there's usually good fishing there. I'll run up to the tower and look. You can see way down the beach from there."

She scuttled up the narrow, winding stairs—scarcely more than a twisting ladder—with Ted at her heels. Monsieur had decided not to attempt the ascent. Climbing stairs always made him lose his breath. Marty had pushed open the trapdoor that led into the octagonal tower and hurried to one of its windows. She had heard Ted, behind her, almost gasp at the wide view they had of beach, ocean, woods, and farther bay. But her eye had caught the figure of Mr. Burnett, quietly fishing a mile or more farther down, and the two unwelcome visitors trudging disconsolately through the sand, nearer at hand.

"They can't see your father," she had pointed out to Ted. "We can, but he's sort of around a bend in the shore and out of their sight. It's all right! They'll be safely rowing across the bay in a few moments—and probably mad enough that they've had all this trouble for nothing! It's getting late. Let's go down now and go home to see how they got on with Nana."

"This is a strange room," Ted had remarked, as they were preparing to descend. "Did they watch out for wrecks from here?"

"Yes," said Marty. "When the crew was here, they always kept a man in the tower, day and night. He not only had to watch out for wrecks but to report on every vessel that passed along the coast, or anything that he saw around here that was out-of-the-way, like fires in the woods and things like that. We're going to miss them a lot."

"Then why did they send them away and close up the place?" Ted had demanded curiously.

"I'm not sure," replied Marty. "Uncle Cy knows all about it. I think the government decided it wasn't necessary any longer to have so many of them—one every three miles. So they closed up some in between and left the work to the rest. There's another station about six miles down from here that has a full crew. That's supposed to take care of all this region."

Presently they rejoined Monsieur, who had descended to the ground floor.

"But I can guess pretty well what happened when the Kilroys

called," chuckled Marty, "because this isn't the first time things have gone that way! To put it in four words—Nana saw them first! And then she probably did just what we did over at the station. Otherwise, they wouldn't have gone back so soon! She was probably sitting up in that little tower room. She likes to do that sometimes in nice weather. There's a grand view from there, too. Almost as good as the station tower. She has a comfortable little chair there and takes her sewing or the papers and can see all that's going on. She must have seen them coming over from the beach and went down and locked the doors, as if we were all out. Then she went back upstairs again, and she was probably chuckling at their disappointment!"

And this, too, proved a correct surmise, as they had found on their return. Mrs. Greene was in the kitchen, nodding sleepily over the papers, her spectacles well down toward the end of her nose. Thusy also was sound asleep, his head tucked under his wing. The old lady chuckled when they asked her how she'd got on with her visitors, and merely remarked:

"I wasn't 'at home' today! I never am if I see them first—perfect nuisances they are—and always have been!"

There had been one other memory of that evening that Marty was now recalling. After supper, Mr. Burnett had suggested that they walk over to the beach and watch the moon rise, as it must be even then about due to appear over the ocean. A deep afterglow still tinted the west as they passed through the lane, and as they emerged over the dunes, a great orange disk was slowly edging up over the eastern horizon, painting a broad path of light on the quiet ocean. Ted had walked ahead with Monsieur, and Mr. Burnett had laid a detaining hand for a moment on Marty's arm.

"Tell me," he had said, "what are you doing with Ted? He's been like a different boy this evening! I couldn't help but notice it. His eyes were bright, he smiles and laughs in his old, natural way—and I even noticed he ate every scrap of his supper and asked for more. What have you done?" And then Marty had told him, as much as she could in the short time they had, what her plan had been in getting him interested in the mystery that seemed to surround the blue macaw.

"Marvelous!" he had cried. "I couldn't have thought of anything half so intriguing. Why, you've even got me deeply interested in it myself! And I venture to predict that it's going to take Ted so out of himself that he'll have very little time to consider his own worries—and sorrows. You have my eternal gratitude, Marty!"

She had just reached this point in her review of the past evening and could see the Coast Guard station tower very near and eerily appearing and disappearing in the thick, surrounding mist. Suddenly she was startled by a figure plunging out of the bushes directly in her path.

"Why, Ted!" she gasped. "What in the world are you doing here?" The boy had on a thick sweater, but his head was bare, and his curly dark hair was beaded with moisture. His big blue eyes were alight with excitement.

"I wanted to catch you, Marty, before you got home," he panted. "I've got something awfully important to tell you! Can you come over to the station with me for a while?"

"Why, of course!" answered Marty, wonderingly. "But why were you in the bushes? Why didn't you just walk up the road?"

"Because—" he hesitated, "because your cousin Gwen has been—sort of—hanging around—and teasing me. And I didn't want her to know what we're going to do."

"Gwen's been teasing you? She would!" commented Marty bitterly. "She's the most awful little tease I ever knew! But how was she teasing you, Ted?"

"Well—" he hesitated again. "I don't like to tell tales on her. I hate that kind of thing. I began practicing this morning, and then we came over to the station again this afternoon, Monsieur and I, for a little practice. But it was sort of dark and damp there, and the pianos got a bit out of tune with this fog and dampness. So Monsieur decided to give it up for today. He went off to fish with

Dad and told me I'd better go back to the house. But there was something I'd discovered that was rather interesting in the station this morning, and I wanted to stop and look it over some more—and show it to you. So I asked him to lock up the front door and take the key, and I'd stay around a while and go out by the back door and take that key myself.

"And that's what we did. He went off, and I stayed around till it was nearly time for you to come home. Then I went out and locked up the kitchen door. But just as I came around the station toward the road, there was Gwen coming home from school. She ran up to me and began to chatter a lot. And then she asked me if my name was Theodore. I told her it was but that I preferred to be called 'Ted.' But she said she was going to call me 'Dora.' I said I wished she wouldn't, please. You see, when I went to boarding school, the boys, some of them, used to call me Dora and—and say I was a sissy. I'm not a sissy—and I hate it all so!" He gulped, and Marty's tender heart ached at the thought of the pain it must have caused him. But he went on bravely:

"Well, that didn't seem to make any difference to Gwen, for she began jumping round me shouting, 'Dora—Dora!' at the top of her lungs. No matter which way I turned, I couldn't get away from her—and I did so want to be sure to catch you before you got home. At last I walked away down the lane toward the house. She followed me quite a way, but she got tired of it finally, I guess, and turned and went back. Then I scooted way around through the bushes and bogs and everything till I got out right near the road here. And then you came along."

"I'll see that this doesn't happen again!" said Marty grimly. "I won't tell her what you've told me—don't worry about that! But it'll be about all there is of that sort of thing. Now let's go to the station. I'm anxious to know what you are going to show me."

"That's just the trouble," objected Ted. "She's still hanging around there, waiting to see if I'll come back. I saw her just two or three minutes ago. And I don't want her to know we're going in there. I have a special reason."

"Well, I know what to do about that!" laughed Marty. "We'll go back toward the house through these bushes you came through. Then I know a secret path to get around to the back of the station by. She won't be able to see us through this fog, and we'll just sneak in the kitchen door!"

"Hurray!" cried Ted. "I knew you'd think of a way. Let's go!" And they both turned and plunged into the bushes.

It was very dark and dismal in the station that afternoon. The gray fog whirled by the windows, and only occasionally could one glimpse the white-crested breakers crashing in on the beach. But their dull roar could be heard like a continuous accompaniment. The glass in the windows ran with moisture, and the two grand pianos were closed and shrouded with their rubber covers, as Monsieur had left them.

"What is it you want to show me?" demanded Marty when they had entered and locked the door behind them. "We oughtn't to stay here long. It's too cold and dismal." Ted led the way to a little room off the messroom, which had evidently been used as an office when the station had been in active service. In one corner stood a scarred wooden desk and chair, and against the wall over the desk was a long shelf that had once held a number of tall, bulky volumes. A few of these volumes still remained, leaning together at one end of the shelf. There was nothing else in the bare little room.

"I came in here this morning," began Ted, "after I'd been practicing quite a while, and Monsieur thought I ought to have a rest. I saw those books up on the shelf and took one down to look at it because I didn't have anything else to do. I didn't know what they were, and I wasn't very interested in them at first. But all of a sudden I came across something that made me jump! Do you know what those books are, Marty?"

"Of course," she said indifferently. "I've seen them loads of times, but Uncle Cy would never let me look at them. He was awfully particular about that when he was skipper here. But I never wanted to, anyway, so it didn't matter. Most of them are gone now—all the recent ones. They were packed up and taken to headquarters. They didn't have room for them all that first trip, so they left these very old ones. But I heard Uncle Cy say the other day that they were coming back to take the rest very soon."

"Well, it's good they didn't take *these*," remarked Ted mysteriously, "or we'd probably never have found out something about Thusy!"

"About *Thusy*!" cried Marty incredulously. "Why, whatever could there be in those books about *him*?"

"Just wait till you see!" chuckled Ted, and he scrambled up on the desk and reached for the volume on the end of the row. Then he laid it on the desk, opened it to a certain page, and together they bent over it. Marty was now quite curious to see what the inside of these hitherto forbidden volumes looked like and scanned the page from top to bottom.

It began with a date, "Thursday, February 25, 1900." Then there followed several lines concerning "direction and force of wind and state of weather and surf at midnight, sunrise, noon, and sunset." After that came the thermometer and barometer readings for the same hours. Beneath these came the names of the patrolmen and the hours in which they made their patrols up and down the beach. Under these were a number of questions concerning the station or "house" as it was called in these records. Was it clean? Was it in good repair? Was the apparatus in good condition? How many members of the crew (including keeper) were present? Who was absent, and why? Still farther down were the "ships, barks, brigs, schooners, steamers, and sloops" that had passed the station that day. But all the last third of the page was given to an item called "General Remarks." And it was to this last that Ted excitedly called her attention.

"All the rest don't amount to so much," he cried, "but just you read what's written here! Most of the general remarks on other pages are just something about the winds and tides and that they cleaned the house that day or had a surf-boat drill, or something.

But *this* is different; they must have had a big storm that night, and a wreck! But go ahead and read it—and you'll see what I did!"

Ted's cheeks were brilliant red from excitement, and his eyes fairly sparkled as he pointed out the writing to Marty. And, bending over it, she read aloud:

> "As Watch from 12 midnight to 4 a.m. was on his way back to Station, saw a three-masted schooner ashore on bar. Burnt his Coston light at once and returned to Station. Notified keeper who started with his crew and cart through snowdrifts to the Wreck. Arrived abreast of her about 4 in morning. In places the snow were three feet deep. Made three shots each one falling over the vessel but could not get the line on account of sea breaking over her. Made a fourth shot and it held. Only one man pulled ashore in breeches buoy. He said all the rest of vessel crew swept overboard. Myself, Abner Greene, and Jesse Burdick came near losing our own lives, rescued man had leg broke. Keeping him in Distress Room.
> "ALVIN KILROY, *keeper*"

There was silence in the little room for a moment after Marty ceased reading the record aloud. The fog outside had changed to rain. A heavy northeast wind had sprung up, and the raindrops drummed on the windows in hissing streams. But the two did not notice it.

"Well," remarked Marty at length, "I don't see anything there of special interest to us except those two names. Abner Greene, who must have been number one surfman at that time, was my grandfather, and Alvin Kilroy, the keeper, was the father-in-law of that woman who came over here yesterday. All I can say is that his grammar was terrible and his spelling worse—from the look of this record he wrote. But what has all this got to do with Thusy?"

"But you haven't seen anything—yet!" commented Ted, with a little grin. "Just go on and read the 'General Remarks' for the next day."

Marty hurried to turn the page, and skipping all the other items on the record for February 26th, she gazed at the remarks in question. This time she did not read them aloud, but they ran:

> Vessel referred to yesterday was the *Spindrift* of New Bedford, Mass., bound from Havana to New York with lite cargo, mostly fruit and coconuts. Captain Phineas Grant was Master. He and eight seamen swept overboard before the first line came across. All nine bodies came ashore this a.m. The one rescued in breeches buoy still pretty bad here with broken leg. Had a big canvas bag on his back when we brought him in and in the bag he had a live parrot. Man said his name was Jack Mountain. Will give more in report.
> ALVIN KILROY

This time Ted had scored. Marty's eyes almost popped out of her head as she stuttered:

"A *parrot*!—and—and—a man named '*Jack*!'"

V

MONSIEUR HAS A THEORY

"Well," sighed Marty, when she had sufficiently recovered from her astonishment at this revelation, "you certainly discovered something this time, Ted. But tell me, is there anything more about it in these records?"

"I haven't had time to look," said Ted. "I did look through a few pages, but there wasn't anything. Then I thought I'd wait till you came and we could—"

At this moment there came an interruption. There was a violent knocking on the back kitchen door, which Ted had locked against a possible intrusion by Gwen. It startled both of them, and Marty whispered:

"Who can that be?" She darted to the door and, turning the key, threw it open to behold—Mr. Burnett and Monsieur, thoroughly soaked by the drenching rain.

"We got caught in this downpour," Mr. Burnett explained as they entered. "And on the way back to the house, we thought we'd better stop and see if Ted was still here. He ought to get back before this gets any worse. But what in the world are you two doing in this forlorn, cold place?"

"We've found something awful interesting!" cried Ted, his eyes alight. "About Thusy. Do let us show it to you before we leave here!"

"It was Ted who found it," laughed Marty, "and brought me in to look at it. It certainly *is* strange!" And they both, in breathless sentences, explained to the newcomers what the old records had contained. The news intrigued the older pair quite as much as it had the younger. Wet as they were, they placed their fishing rods in a corner and demanded to see the curious records at once.

"This is very odd, indeed. I think you've struck something, Ted," said Mr. Burnett, when they had both finished the two entries. "I hardly think there can be a doubt that this refers to the same bird Mrs. Greene now has. And as for the sailor who owned him, Jack Mountain, who else could it be that you say Thusy has referred to as 'Jack'? This seems to clinch it. But the question is, what became of Jack, and how did the parrot come into the possession of Mrs. Greene, and why does she not seem to want to talk about it? There's a story behind that, I'm certain!"

"But—ees zis all about heem in zis book?" demanded Monsieur. "Somesing else must have happen to zat Jack. Hees leg, it is broke! How does he get away from here?"

"Let's look through the record a bit further," said Mr. Burnett. "Monsieur and I are wet and cold, and we've all got a bit of a storm to go through before reaching the house. But I can't sleep tonight till we've found out something more."

"Neither can I," announced Ted, and the other two added the same sentiment. So they turned again to the record book, and all bent over it eagerly, scanning the following pages for some hint of the fate of "Jack Mountain." The ensuing "General Remarks" were in the main short and concerned only the usual routine of the station: cleaning and airing the house, having flag drills, practice with the cart, and matters of wind, weather, and tide. But suddenly they all gave a shout, for about seven entries later on, they came upon these short but meaningful sentences:

"Man we brought ashore night of Feb. 25th, no better. Too

stormy ever since to get doctor from mainland. Today number one man, Abner Greene, offered to take him into his house nearby. Said he would be more comfortable there. Jesse Burdick and James Ashmore removed him to Greene's house on a stretcher."

That was all, but from this meager item, the four could instantly build up the story. Jack Mountain and his parrot had undoubtedly been taken into Mrs. Greene's home by herself and her husband. That must explain the origin of Thusy. But what had happened after *that*? What had eventually become of Jack Mountain? Had he stayed there, or did he depart after a while, leaving his pet in Mrs. Greene's possession? And why didn't she want to talk about it? They questioned one another frantically, trying to find an answer to these new queries.

"Why not look through the rest of the records?" Ted finally suggested. "Maybe there's some more about them there." But Mr. Burnett said he thought that quite unlikely. These records, which had to be short because of the space allotted them, seemed to concern only the affairs of the station itself. When anything or anyone passed out of the station's keeping, it was out for good. He did suggest, however, that tomorrow they might do some more research work in this field but that, as the storm was increasing in violence, they had best get back to the house as promptly as possible. They had, at least, discovered the thing it was most essential to know—the manner in which Thusy had been introduced to the Greene household.

And so, Marty having found in a locker an old, discarded sou'wester that she wrapped about Ted, they all scurried through the pelting rain to the house, accompanied by the ominous roar of the surf pounding on the beach behind the dunes.

There was an air of decided gloom about this house when they reached it—a gloom not all attributable to the stormy weather. After the four had changed to dry clothing and were gathered in the warm kitchen, the depression became very apparent. Mrs. Greene was grimly peeling potatoes at the sink, and Thusy was huddled on his perch, curiously silent, his bright plumage appearing rather rumpled.

"What's the matter, Nana?" demanded Marty, automatically taking the peeling knife from Mrs. Greene and continuing the task. "Where's Hettie? Why isn't she doing this?"

"I sent her home just before the rain began," said Mrs. Greene. "I knew it was going to be bad, so she might as well go when she could. I declare, that girl frustrates me so much sometimes! She's willing enough, but she's noisy and so clumsy that she drops or spills just about everything she touches. This afternoon she dropped my best meat platter and broke it all to bits. And I know she's been feeding Thusy on the sly with sweets and things he oughtn't to have, though I told her not to. He's sick, that bird is! Just look at him! And I'm worried to pieces about him!"

It was all too true. Methuselah looked far from his squawking, vigorous self. His usually bright eyes had a glazed appearance, and he sat with his head hunched far down among his shoulder feathers.

They all looked shocked over the state of affairs, and Marty suddenly exclaimed, "Oh! I nearly forgot to tell you—I've had so much else to think about." (And here she looked slyly toward their three guests.) "I haven't got to go to school tomorrow, nor for two weeks probably. Anyway, they sent around word everything is all right. Some sickness has broken out, over across the bay, and they're afraid it might turn into an epidemic, it's so catching. So they've dismissed school till further notice. Now I can be home—isn't that grand? And I won't have any homework to do, so I can help you, Nana, and we won't need to have Hettie Boscom around."

Mrs. Greene looked quite relieved at this news, and Mr. Burnett, who had been warming his hands at the stove, broke in with another suggestion.

"I've a plan to add to that, too, if you'll allow me, Mrs. Greene. I hope you'll allow us three fellows the pleasure of making our own beds and tidying up our rooms. It won't take long every morning, and that'll relieve you and Marty of some of the work. And we'd like to do it!" And, he added, seeing Mrs. Greene's scandalized expression, "Now I do hope you won't object. It will make this just like a glorious camping expedition deluxe. To tell you the truth, I had thought of a *real* camping trip before Professor Sedgwick persuaded us to try this. And in that case, we would have been doing far more work and having a lot more trouble than we'd have here, doing nothing but making our beds! Just for the fun of it, Mrs. Greene, I beg you to let us do this! Will you be so kind?"

Ted and Monsieur promptly joined in his plea, and at last Mrs. Greene, shaking her head over the extraordinary idea, finally gave a grudging consent.

"Hurrah!" cried Ted with sudden enthusiasm. "Now we're going to have real fun!"

Marty and Mr. Burnett glanced at each other covertly, as if to note that the wistful boy of a few days ago was certainly making progress.

"But what about Thusy?" went on Mr. Burnett. "We're terribly sorry to hear he is under the weather. What can be done about it?"

"Oh, he'll get over it, like he usually does," said Mrs. Greene. "Part of it's due to the weather. He always acts sort of low spirited during a northeaster. He don't like 'em! But I caught Hettie only yesterday just about to give him a piece of apple pie left from one of the plates, and I just *know* she's given him other things he oughtn't to have. The way I treat him for this is to take away all of his food for a day or so—just give him a little fresh water. Then he comes out of it."

"Just a case of too high living," laughed Mr. Burnett. "Well, let's hope it won't bother him long!"

"It surely is odd," thought Marty that night at the jolly supper table while the storm raged outside, "I've only known these people a few days, but I feel as well acquainted with them as if I'd known them all my life! I never knew before that there *could* be such friendly folks. Nana must feel the same way, too. I never knew her to talk so freely to almost strangers before—except Professor Sedgwick."

The conversation turned to the storm and the wild ocean. And before Marty quite realized it, Mr. Burnett had steered the talk toward the subject of the Coast Guard service and the dangerous and difficult work it must have been, especially in past years when there were few facilities, such as roads and communication, on this wild beach.

"By the way, Mrs. Greene," he suddenly remarked, "I understand your husband was once skipper of this station. He must have had some rather hair-raising experiences in that capacity, with storms and wrecks!"

"Yes, he did," she agreed with what, for her, was surprising communicativeness. "He near lost his life more'n once. I used to worry so about him that my hair started turning gray when I was only thirty. And when he died, it was in the line of duty—in one of these terrible storms." She hesitated a bit, and her voice quivered as she made this statement. A rather embarrassed pause followed, which Mr. Burnett broke by commenting:

"A brave man—and a great pity that his life had to be sacrificed! But, by the way, we came across a rather singular thing over at the station this afternoon. We were in there when the storm began and were looking over some of those old Coast Guard records they still have stored there—and mighty interesting reading they make! But one item we stumbled on quite surprised us, for it told of a wreck one winter night about thirty-five or more years ago, in which a single sailor was brought in to shore in the breeches buoy, and with him, he had a live parrot in a canvas bag. It seems his leg had been broken—the sailor's, I mean!—during the affair, and after keeping him at the station a few days, he was taken to the home of a surfman named Abner Greene. The coincidence was so complete that we couldn't help but guess that it must have been this very Thusy. I wonder if we were right?"

Marty and the others secretly gasped at his temerity in asking this question. And Mrs. Greene herself looked rather stunned for a moment. Then she faltered:

"Oh! Did Alvin Kilroy put all that in the record? Well, yes, it was Thusy! That's how he come to be here—to begin with. The man that owned him—he called himself Jack Mountain, or just Sailor Jack—he was awful bad off for a while with a broken leg. My husband couldn't bear to see him suffering at the station—they didn't have no real comfortable place for him there—so he offered to take him to the house till he got well. We got a doctor for him when the weather let up enough to get one from 'crost the bay. But his leg never did heal up right. The doctor said he'd probably walk lame the rest of his life—and so he did."

"It was mighty kind of you to take him in and give him good care," commented Mr. Burnett. "And he left his parrot with you when he finally went away?" They all held their breath, waiting for her response to this.

"It's a good thing it's Mr. Burnett asking these questions and not me," thought Marty. "Nana would never tell *me* a thing about this!"

"Well, matter of fact," hesitated Mrs. Greene, "he never *did* leave. After he got well enough to—and that took a long while—he said he never could go back to be a sailor, with his leg like it was, and he didn't know what else to do. Said he liked it here so much with us that, if we'd be willing to keep him on as a boarder, he'd be glad to stay. Said he'd pay good board, too, and help around the place. Said he was getting too old to work steadily anymore and would be glad to have a regular home, and he didn't know a nicer place than this was. So, we let him stay." She stopped there, as if that were the end of the tale.

But her listeners were still bursting with urgent questions, and Mr. Burnett voiced one of them: "This is most interesting, Mrs. Greene! But isn't it rather singular that he could pay you so well—and indefinitely? A common sailor's wages aren't large and usually don't last very long. I wonder how he came to have so much?"

"He seemed to have plenty," she agreed, "though where it come from I dunno! He brought a large canvas bag strapped to his back when he come ashore, and I guess Thusy wasn't the only thing in it! We never asked him about that. It wasn't any of our business so long as he paid his board."

"But—what kind of man ees he?" put in Monsieur, excitedly. "Do he speak zee Eengleesh well? Do he talk in any ozzer language?"

Mrs. Greene sent him a startled look. Then she acknowledged, "He—he did speak English—quite well—just like anybody else. But he used to talk to Thusy in some other language. I dunno—I guess it must have been—French!"

"I knew eet—I knew eet!" shouted Monsieur, running his hands wildly through his hair. "Zat bird—he know zee language—he remember eet—" Suddenly he stopped short, thought a moment, and announced dramatically, "Zat name he have, 'Jack Mountain,' zat ees no *French* name! But me, I suddenly think, 'Jack Mountain?' Eet sound like zee French '*Jacques Montagne*.' Zat ees what eet surely ees! Now I know zat man—he ees really French!"

"Mebbe he was," said Mrs. Greene shortly, rising to clear the table, as the meal was long since finished. "It sounds pretty much the same to me."

Monsieur and Ted strolled over to where Thusy was dozing on his perch by the warm fire, and Monsieur began talking softly to him in French. The ailing bird presently opened his still somewhat glazed eyes and began to rock slightly from side to side on his perch. Plainly the warmth and coziness of the room, as well as the cheerful company about him, were beginning to revive his drooping spirits. Thusy always hated to be alone, especially on a gloomy day.

Suddenly, under the spell of the murmured French, he began to chuckle softly, a weirdly human-sounding chuckle. After several moments of this, he rose on his perch, flapped his wings feebly, and opened his bill, squawking:

"*Vive le roi!—Vive le roi!—Vive—*" And just as suddenly, he lapsed once more into his drowsy attitude of the earlier evening and was silent.

"Bravo!" cried Monsieur, delighted with the result of his experiment. "Zat ees somesing else he remember!"

"Wh—what does it mean?" stammered Marty, in startled wonder.

"It means, 'Long live the King!'" shouted Ted. "I know *that*!"

Mrs. Greene, stacking dishes at the kitchen sink, said nothing. She felt that she had said far too much already that evening. But Monsieur, rubbing his hands together and chuckling gleefully, remarked:

"Eet means—zat bird—hees memory—eet *wake up*!"

VI

ONE MEMORABLE DAY

Old Mrs. Greene was stepping about her kitchen, preparing vegetables for the midday meal. The early morning sun streamed in at the south window, and the kitchen was at its brightest hour of the day. Methuselah, on his perch, was pecking half-heartedly at the sunflower seeds in his cup. Having recovered somewhat from his indisposition of the day before, he was being allowed a limited ration of food, but his appetite was still far from normal.

It was plain that the old lady was mentally upset. There were tears streaming down her furrowed cheeks—not, however, from her mental state, but from the onions she was peeling at the sink. Presently she wiped her eyes with a corner of her apron and muttered:

"I dunno what possessed me last night! I must've been crazy to talk so much—telling things like that to plain strangers! They're nice enough folks—but I dunno how I got led into it. Trouble is, I said too much—and yet not enough! I wouldn't never had said anything if it hadn't been they'd found out so much from—"

"Don't get excited!—Don't get excited!—Don't get—" suddenly

squawked Thusy, inspired no doubt by Mrs. Greene's audible mutterings.

"Looka here!" exclaimed the exasperated old lady, approaching the bird. "I have enough to worry me without you making that pesky racket. If you don't keep quiet, Thusy, sure as I stand here, I'll put you in your cage and throw the black shawl over it. You hear me?"

The parrot eyed her a moment as if digesting her threat. Then he maliciously winked one eye and screeched, "Go fly a kite!— Go fly—" But before she could carry out the threat, he returned suddenly and quietly to his seed cup, and silence reigned once more.

Mrs. Greene turned to shake down the ashes in the range and put the onions on to boil. Fearing to rouse Thusy to action once more, she did no further muttering aloud, but inwardly she was thinking, "There ain't no manner of use! I can't let it go like that. I ain't going to have 'em thinking—"

She did not finish the sentence, even in her own mind. Reaching into the closet for a basket, she let herself out into the garden to see if there were any ripe tomatoes left on her vines after the storm of the previous night.

Meanwhile, Mr. Burnett and Marty were bouncing—literally bouncing!—out through the lane and along the narrow sand-rut road in Mr. Burnett's big car, on their way to Surf Crest, the little summer town that had grown up on the northern end of Heron Shoals Island. They both had errands to do. Marty was to tell Hettie Boscom that she was not needed at the Greene ménage for the present, and to do some marketing. Mr. Burnett wanted his mail and the daily papers, and he also had another errand of which he had not spoken.

The morning had dawned clear but distinctly breezy after the storm of the night before. The wind was still strongly northeast, what Mrs. Greene called a "dry northeaster," but with the result of a pellucidly clear atmosphere, rain-washed, cool, and perfect for being outdoors. Due to the bouncing and swaying of the car, neither of its occupants had any breath or desire for conversation till they struck the surfaced roadway at the southern end of the town. Then Mr. Burnett settled back comfortably in the driving seat, smiled at Marty beside him, and began:

"Some rough road—that! But be thankful for it, Marty. It's one very effective barrier that keeps your lovely wild beach from being invaded by too many unwelcome visitors. But now that we've regained our breath, I want to tell you about a plan I've made for this afternoon. It's such a grand day for the thing that I want to take advantage of it. Here's the scheme:

"After we've finished the errands, I plan to drive to Captain Bell's place close by on the bay. He has a small motorboat there that I've arranged to hire for the day sometime. We'll leave the car at his place, take the motorboat, and chug down the bay to the nearest spot to your house and carry our supplies back from there. Then, after dinner, I want to take you and Monsieur and Ted on a trip down the bay. It's a particularly good day to go because, though the wind is quite high on the ocean side, it will be fairly calm over on the bay, especially if we keep as close as possible to the shore. I have two reasons for making this trip. The most important is to visit the Coast Guard station down near South Inlet. I particularly want Ted to see it because he's been asking me so many questions about how the stations are run when they are in regular working order. The boat and flag drills, the breeches-buoy drill, and how the big boat room looks, and all that sort of thing. I thought it would divert him and do him a lot of good to visit that one. And, while we're working down the bay, Monsieur and I might do some trolling if we take our fishing lines along. How does this strike you?"

"Why, it's awfully kind of you to ask me to go along," said Marty, her eyes shining at the prospect. "I like to go out on the bay, but I don't get much chance to nowadays. I know every shoal and channel of it hereabouts, too, so perhaps I can direct you. Sometimes people who are strangers to it get stuck badly out on the flats if they don't know where they are. And I think it will be grand for Ted, too. Help him think about—other things."

"Well, I'm so glad you like the prospect," agreed Mr. Burnett. "Since you know the best course to take, you shall do the steering, if you care to. I'll tend to the motor."

Thrilled with the proposed adventure, Marty rushed through her errands, and they drove to the dock near North Inlet, on the bay, where old Captain Bell had his motorboat for hire. Leaving the car locked near the dock, they removed Marty's purchases to the boat—a small one that drew as little water as possible. And with a rowboat hitched at the stern, they skimmed out into the bay on the homeward trip, Marty secretly thrilled with pride at being allowed to do the steering, while Mr. Burnett tinkered a while with the unfamiliar motor down in the tiny cockpit.

Having passed the town, they began to slip by the wide salt meadows edging the bay in that locality, and Mr. Burnett emerged to sit nearby, while Marty expertly steered the boat through some baffling channels between the many sandy shoals. Shortly after they drew closer to the shore, now beginning to be lined, close to the water's edge, with thick-growing cedars and blossoming groundsel bushes. The water was very calm and smooth near the shore, and their little boat made but a comparatively faint sound as it cut its way through the blue water. Innumerable swallows flicked through the air. A crested kingfisher, perched on a stump, flew off at their approach. A flock of red-winged blackbirds rose from a reed-grown point. Suddenly they spied a great blue heron, standing immovable in the shallows near the shore, his long bill poised to snap up some unwary fish. He must have stood nearly five feet tall. Mr. Burnett shut off the motor so that he might not be alarmed, but he had seen them even before it was done. With a mighty flap of his great wings, he rose awkwardly and sailed away through the blue sky, his long legs trailing behind him.

"What a beautiful specimen!" sighed Mr. Burnett. "Are there

many of them around here?"

"Oh, lots!" said Marty, twisting the steering wheel to send them out around a long point of land. "'Specially down farther, along our region. Nana told me that's why this island was called 'Heron Shoals,' because there were so many blue herons here and the water is so shallow along the shore of the bay."

Rather abruptly, Mr. Burnett changed the subject. "There's one angle of our mystery that has puzzled me a good deal, a point we haven't been giving much attention to, and that's these Kilroys and what connection they have with it all. Just what do you know about them, Marty? You never got a chance to tell me very much."

Marty gave him an account similar to the one she had given Ted, but she could add little enlightenment as to their connection with the mystery of Thusy. She also told him a bit about the young lad whom she called "Chips Kilroy."

"It's too bad about him," she explained. "I think he would be quite a nice boy if only his mother hadn't spoiled his disposition by nagging and bossing him about. She's made him so ugly that he can't get along with anyone hardly. Keeps him home from school doing chores for her so that he misses half his work. That's how he got that nickname, Chips, because the only excuse he'd give when he'd been absent was that he had to chop wood for his mother. The boys at school call him 'Chips Killjoy,' but mostly just 'Killjoy'—and he hates it!"

"I should think he would, and it's a great pity," sympathized Mr. Burnett. "It's enough to sour anyone's disposition! But what led me to this subject was a letter I received from Professor Sedgwick this morning. He had written to ask how we were enjoying our stay here and to give me some good suggestions on fishing matters in this locality. But, incidentally, he slid in something about these Kilroys, and I'd like to read that part of his letter to you."

Mr. Burnett searched among his mail and papers and drew out a letter, which he opened, and found the paragraphs in question. Then he began to read aloud:

"I wonder, have you come in contact with the curious Kilroys from across the bay yet? I mention them because they are occasional visitors to Mrs. Greene—not very welcome ones either. Mrs. G apparently detests them—for reasons I have never been able to ascertain definitely. But I had one rather curious encounter with them a few years ago, which it might interest you to hear about. It happened this way:

"I wasn't feeling at all well one hot Saturday morning and had decided to stay in the house instead of going fishing. Mrs. G and Marty had gone up to town on some errands, leaving me alone in the house. I had elected to sit in the parlor, as it was cooler there and had less mosquitoes than on the veranda. I had been reading but must have fallen into a doze, for presently I came to myself and heard voices out in the kitchen. Thinking Mrs. G and Marty must have returned, I paid no attention at first. But suddenly I realized that those were not the voices of the Greenes. One was a high, rather shrill female voice, and the other sounded more like a grumpy boy's. But there were none that sounded like Mrs. G's or Marty's.

"Thinking it all rather strange, and that perhaps I'd better investigate these intruders, I tiptoed out to the hall to hear a little better what was being said. The first remark I got clearly was from the woman, saying it was evident Mrs. G was not home—and that for once she'd left the place alone and unlocked. And she ended by saying this would be *a good time to look*—and that they'd never get a better. The boy replied in a rather surly fashion that he wasn't going to do it—and that they'd better go right home, or else wait for the Greenes to return.

"Well, you can imagine I was rather startled by all

this and considered it high time I intervened. So, I tiptoed back into the parlor and then walked out rather noisily down the hall and into the kitchen. They were a pretty startled pair when they saw me, but I only inquired, quite blandly, and as if I'd heard nothing, whether they'd come to see Mrs. Greene, and could I do anything for them, as she was out and would be gone for some time. They hastily assured me that they were friends from across the bay (at least, the woman did, the boy said nothing!). They had, she said, come over to Heron Shoals on some other business and thought that, while here, they'd drop in for a visit to the Greenes. Finding the house open, she had thought the family were only away a short distance and that they would wait. But as their time was limited, and as Mrs. G would not be back very soon, they had better go on at once. And would I kindly leave their regard for the Greenes. They thereupon beat a hasty retreat, acting considerably flustered and probably wondering how much I'd overheard!

"Then he went on," continued Mr. Burnett, "to sketch for me what he'd found out about these people from Mrs. Greene when she got back. As it's practically the same as what you've told me, I won't bother to read it. He ended by saying he has always been a good deal puzzled by the mystery of the visit—and wonders still what they were about to 'look for,' as they'd said. He remarked that Mrs. Greene had never enlightened him on that point. That's all, but it has made me think that it might be a good idea to look into this matter more carefully, and I have rather a notion where we can begin."

"Oh, *where*?" cried Marty, almost grounding the boat on the sandy shoal in her excitement.

"In those Coast Guard record books!" he answered. "And I'm

going to start this very morning, as soon as we get back—even if it means giving up some hours of fishing. Ted and Monsieur are over at the station practicing, but I'll slip in and do my sleuthing in the little office, where it won't interrupt them. And, by the way, we're nearly opposite the house now. I can see the cupola above the trees. Take her as near the shore as you can, Marty, without grounding her. We'll anchor her there, load our things into the rowboat, and paddle ashore. I'm leaving her all set for our afternoon jaunt."

Shortly thereafter, they were trudging through the woods along the sandy path toward the house, heavily loaded down with bundles of groceries. It was rather a long pull, and they were fairly out of breath when they reached their destination.

An hour or so later, having finished with her duties around the house, Marty rambled over to the station, unable any longer to contain her curiosity. She entered the back kitchen door and saw Mr. Burnett seated at the desk in the little office, a record book before him on the desk. He was not, however, examining it but was simply sitting there with a faraway look in his eyes, listening to the flood of music from the messroom. Marty, too, stopped short to listen to the exquisite notes coming from one of the pianos. She was sure it must be Monsieur who was playing till she glanced in and saw the little Frenchman standing by one of the windows, beating time softly with his hand—and Ted at the piano! It was the first time she had heard the boy play, and she was startled at this evidence of his very great gift. So full and true and mature was his rendering that Marty could not help but whisper, half aloud:

"Why—he plays like a—like a *real* artist!"

Mr. Burnett looked up and saw her. "Yes, he is a real artist, even at this early age. I'm convinced of that. This—that he's playing—was his mother's favorite."

"It's the Chopin A-flat Major Polonaise—isn't it?" ventured Marty. Mr. Burnett looked astonished.

"Why, forgive me," he exclaimed, "but how do you come to know so much about classical music, Marty?"

The girl blushed in some embarrassment. "Oh, I don't know much—but I like it. You see, in our school, we've listened to those Music Appreciation hours on Friday afternoons that are given by a great conductor in New York on the radio. I like them—best of anything we learn. We have to keep notebooks about what we hear and show how well we remember the things that are played. I won a prize last year for having the best and most correct notebook—but it's only because I like music so much," she ended shyly.

"Well, I think that's simply remarkable," said Mr. Burnett. "I remember we were never taught interesting things like that when *I* went to school. Times certainly have changed!"

The music in the other room had ceased, and Monsieur was explaining some technical point to his pupil. Suddenly Mr. Burnett turned to the Coast Guard journal that lay before him.

"But I want you to see something I've just discovered," he went on, pointing to the open page. "I think we've found something that explains a great deal!"

VII

FOOTPRINTS IN THE SAND

IT HAD BEEN A GLORIOUS afternoon. As Marty looked back on it afterward, it was also the last afternoon they were to know of quiet enjoyment and freedom from worry, bewilderment, and even danger, for some time to come.

The trip down the bay in the motorboat had been delightful. The wind of the earlier hours had completely died away, leaving an almost dead calm. The boat had slipped through the mirror-like water, her prow cutting a wide, triangular swath of ripples. Monsieur and Mr. Burnett had cast their trolling lines over the stern, leaving Marty and Ted to do the steering, and their efforts had resulted in two small bluefish, or snappers, with which catch they were inordinately delighted. The quiet, uninhibited shores had slipped by till at last they were opposite the Coast Guard station, where they were able to hitch their boat to the end of a little dock that projected out from the shore.

Ted had found his visit to this full-crew station absorbing. Under the guidance of its kindly skipper, they had explored it from end to end and top to bottom—had been shown the big boat room, witnessed a flag drill, had the breeches buoy and its drill explained to them, climbed to the tower to talk with the man on duty, watched him check the passing vessels on a blackboard, and finally were treated to cups of cocoa and huge ham sandwiches in the mess room.

Before they left, the skipper remarked, "I hope you get back before the fog comes up. See it—out there on the ocean—piled low on the horizon? The barometer's falling, too. Guess we haven't seen the last of that storm we had last night. Wind swung around the wrong way before she dropped this afternoon. Generally means the storm's coming back again."

"I noticed in this morning's paper that there's a hurricane hanging around off the Florida coast," commented Mr. Burnett. "I hope it doesn't take it into its head to turn and come up this way!"

"No fear!" laughed the skipper. "This is just some of the contrary weather we sometimes get here around the last of September. But it often can be *mean*."

Then they were back in the boat, the warm sun still shining, the water as unruffled as before. But beyond the dunes to the east, and now rising well above them, an opalescent mist was beginning to bulk higher and higher.

"Better streak it straight for home, Marty!" commented Mr. Burnett. "It's so calm now that we won't have to hug the shore. I believe you said there's a channel fairly well out that's more direct. I don't like the look of that rising fog bank. Wouldn't be so pleasant to be caught out on the bay in it!"

Marty obediently shifted a course directly out to the channel, and with the rowboat trailing behind, they settled down to the homeward journey, all pleasantly tired and rather quiet after their day.

Presently Ted remarked, "That's an odd thing you found in the old record this morning, Dad. You made a copy of it, didn't you? I'd like to see it again. Somehow I can't understand what it all means."

Mr. Burnett fished a notebook from his pocket, but before he handed it to his son, he commented, "I've been thinking quite a lot about that record since we found it this morning. Somehow, I'd rather suspected we might come across some item there that would be enlightening, though I didn't figure what it might be. This seems to confirm the suspicion, but even yet, it is only a guess.

"In looking over these record or log books—and I've examined several—I noticed that much of the time during that period when this Kilroy was keeper, the daily record was written up by someone whose handwriting was very good, almost what we used to call 'copperplate,' but at the end was signed by 'Alvin Kilroy, keeper,' whose handwriting was often appallingly poor. I have an idea this was contrary to the rules, as I've understood that it is the duty of the keeper himself to write up the log, except in cases where he is away on leave. But I also noticed that whenever there was a wreck or rescue work to be reported, Kilroy always wrote the whole affair himself. We might draw two conclusions from this. Either Kilroy was too lazy to bother writing all the reports himself—except under special conditions—or perhaps he was ashamed of his handwriting. In all probability, it was the former reason.

"I also noticed that in the volume of the year after the one where we found the record of 'Sailor Jack's' rescue, his writing was growing steadily worse, more careless and blotty. Then you remember that page I pointed out to you all this morning, written up by Kilroy, full of blots and scrawls and things crossed out and put in the wrong sections till the whole thing was practically illegible? It is just a few days after this that I came across the rather startling statement I showed you and copied down. Here's what it said, as you remember." And he read from the notebook:

> "Jessie Burdick on duty during the day. Fresh to east winds at midnight, with stormy weather and rough seas and wind continued fresh until later afternoon. Surf rough all day till sunset. Two full patrols made during day. No shipping seen. Keeper Alvin Kilroy relieved of

his post permanently. No. 1 man, Abner Greene, acting as keeper. Jesse Burdick as No. 1.

"ABNER GREENE,
"Acting keeper"

"But what does it all mean?" interrupted Ted, a puzzled frown on his intent face. "What has it got to do with Thusy—and Sailor Jack?"

"That's what we've got to figure out," explained his father. "Undoubtedly it means that for some special dereliction of duty—or perhaps a whole series of them—Alvin Kilroy had been either demoted or dropped from the service. And Abner Greene had taken his place as acting keeper. This writing was in that fine handwriting, I noticed, and it must have been done by Abner Greene because his name is signed in the same writing. Looking further along in the same record book, I found that about a month later, there was this item in the 'General Remarks':

"'Abner Greene took charge of this station today as keeper, having been properly appointed.'

"What caused the dismissal of Alvin Kilroy, we can't even guess. But one thing it does suggest is that here we have the groundwork for the feud that seems to have existed ever since between the Greenes and the Kilroys. Kilroy was dismissed, and Abner Greene was given his place. And that may very well have been a bitter pill for the Kilroys. Don't you agree with me, Marty?"

"Yes, I do think it's likely," she assented, and added anxiously, "but, Mr. Burnett, isn't there something the matter with that engine? It doesn't sound right to me!"

Mr. Burnett guiltily shoved his notebook into his pocket and dived down into the little cockpit. "You're perfectly right, Marty," he exclaimed, after listening to the explosions of the motor for a moment or two. "She's 'missing' badly, and if I'd been tending to my business, I should have heard it when it first began. I don't know much about motorboat engines, and I do hope this one isn't going to act balky. Captain Bell assured me it was running perfectly and that I wouldn't have a bit of trouble."

"I don't know anything about the workings of them either," declared Marty, "or I'd try to help you out. I can steer a motorboat and start and stop it, but that's about all. Uncle Cy taught me that much."

"Well, I wish Captain Cy were here right now," said Mr. Burnett mournfully as, in spite of his tinkering, the motor sputtered once or twice, coughed dismally, and stopped dead.

"Ees she out of zee gas?" cried Monsieur, anxious to help if only with a suggestion.

"Not a chance," declared Mr. Burnett. "She was full up when I took her out this morning, and she's still two-thirds full. I just looked in the tank. No, it's something I don't understand—and there's plenty I don't understand about these marine engines!" He was still fussing with the various gadgets and getting plentifully smeared with grease in the process.

"She always was a cranky little boat," commented Marty. "I've heard more people complain about her when they've hired her! She runs all right for Captain Bell, but not often for anyone else."

"I wish I'd known that this morning," moaned Mr. Burnett, emerging from the cockpit with grimy hands and a black streak across his forehead. "About how far are we from home, Marty?"

"A little more than halfway," she asserted, looking toward the shore landscape for guidance. "We're just about off Burnt Point, and that's two and a half miles from the house—along the shore."

"Well, the only thing I can see to do," declared Mr. Burnett, "is to anchor her here offshore, get into the rowboat, and row the rest of the way. It'll be a pull, but it's better than being marooned out here! When we get back, I'll walk up to town, tell Captain Bell he'll have to send for his cranky little craft, and then come back in the car."

At this moment the sun was suddenly blotted out, and Ted said, "Look at that fog! It's been rising so that it's even shut out the sun.

We were so busy with other things that we didn't even notice how fast it was coming up!"

All four of them stared about them in considerable dismay, for it was quite as Ted had said. A light southeast wind had sprung up, bringing in the fog more quickly from the ocean. Already the shore of the bay was dim with mist, and the sun was only to be discerned at intervals, soon to be shut out entirely by the misty clouds that were rolling higher and higher.

"Here's a pretty fix!" half-grinned Mr. Burnett. "Drop the anchor, Marty, and if it doesn't hold, we'll have to pole her in nearer the shore." Marty dropped the anchor, and the water being fairly shallow, it held securely. Then Mr. Burnett closed the cockpit and commanded that all get into the boat as speedily as possible.

Hauling up the rowboat, they scrambled in. And as there was only one pair of oars, Mr. Burnett elected to do the rowing. Presently they were all well away from the motorboat, and in a few moments, the fast-rising fog had hidden it from sight. It seemed incredible that half an hour before, they should have been chugging along in carefree cheerfulness, a bright sun and a flat calm promising no apparent reason for alarm. Now they were being rapidly cloaked in a warm, moist mist, the shore shut out, and little or nothing to guide them in the direction they must pursue.

"Better make straight for the shore," advised Marty. "We can follow it along, and then we won't lose our direction. It'll be a longer row, but it'll be safer."

They had been at some distance from the shore when they had anchored the motorboat, and the southeast wind had driven them out a bit farther when the rowing had begun. Mr. Burnett had been pulling steadily on his right oar to turn them in nearer the shore, and at Marty's advice, he now turned more sharply toward the direction of land and pulled with might and main for what seemed a long interval. But only the fog surrounded them, and no shoreline emerged from it.

"Shouldn't we be there soon?" he inquired at last, rather anxiously. "I do hope we are not going in the wrong direction!"

"The shore dips in pretty far, right around here," replied Marty. "You see, we were way out beyond that long point of land, and we drifted out a little farther yet before we got started. So it's quite a bit of a row in. We *should* be going in the right direction, but we can't see a thing now, so I just don't know."

Mr. Burnett jerked at his right oar and tried to keep the small boat on a steady course, rowing on in silence for a time. But still no shore emerged. Presently, he remarked, with a sort of grim humor: "Never again will I be caught out in *any* boat without some sort of a compass! If we had even a small one, we could—"

"*Compass?*" said Ted. "Why didn't I think of it before? The skipper down at the station gave me a tiny little one this afternoon, just to keep in my pocket. He said he had several—and this was an old one—but I could have it if I'd like it!" He searched about in the pocket of his trousers and produced a tiny pocket compass, scarcely more than an inch and a half in diameter, and handed it to his father, who held both oars in one hand for a moment to take it.

"Well, Ted," he remarked with a wry smile, "it's plain to be seen you're no natural sailor or you'd have produced this long ago! However, better late than never, and I think it will be a lifesaver, even if it is scarcely more than a toy. If it tells us which direction is north, that's all we want to know. Can you work it, Marty? I don't dare let this boat drift out any farther."

He handed the instrument to Marty, who turned and twisted it till she had the jiggly little needle directly at the letter N. Then she exclaimed:

"Good *gracious*! We're not going north—or even east—but directly *south*! Now, how in the world can that have happened, exactly the opposite direction?"

"Nothing's more confusing than a thick fog," declared Mr. Burnett, "and this *is* thick!" He pulled the boat around, pointed it due east, and ordered Marty to watch the compass every moment, and if she found them veering off an easterly course, to tell him at once. After a time, they certainly must come to some land.

They rowed on in a rather grim silence, punctuated only by Marty's commands of "right" or "left," if the boat veered off its course. To all of them, it seemed as if, blanketed as they were by the thick, woolly fog, they were cut off from all the world. All were equally startled when a dim line of fog-draped cedars appeared suddenly out of the mist, and the boat grounded on a shallow near the shore. Just what locality they had struck even Marty could not tell, but she suggested that Mr. Burnett let her row for a while, as he must be pretty tired of pulling by this time, particularly as he wasn't used to it.

"I hate to admit it," he laughed in relief, "but my arms *are* rather lame! You row a little while, Marty, and then I'll change with you again. Keep within sight of shore as much as possible, and I'll man the compass." They changed seats, and Marty pushed off, rowing with short, strong strokes that showed her native training.

Having at least sighted land, the party grew more cheerful, realizing that at the worst, they could always go ashore and tramp the rest of the way if they had to.

"I was a bit worried," Marty admitted, "before Ted remembered about that compass. You see, not knowing where we were heading, we might have found ourselves in the middle of the bay before long. The tide is pretty strong there, and before we knew it, we might have drifted into South Inlet. We could have been swept out to sea, and no one would have seen us! I didn't want to tell you that—while we were in danger."

"It might have been pretty serious," agreed Mr. Burnett. "Thank the Lord the skipper gave you that compass, Ted! It saved the day. I didn't see him do it, or I'd have remembered about it myself."

They crept along interminably past the dim, mist-shrouded shores, their way made much longer by the ins and outs of their course around deep coves or long points that jutted out to bar them. The little boat, which scarcely seated two with comfort, was heavily loaded with four, and twice Mr. Burnett and Marty changed places at the rowing seat. Monsieur and Ted had both offered to row, but Mr. Burnett would not hear of that. Their sensitive "piano hands" must not be subjected to the hampering blisters his own were rapidly acquiring. Monsieur had been very silent. The presence of danger seemed to have quenched his usual bubbling loquacity.

Suddenly Marty exclaimed, pushing toward the shore, "Look! That's the next cove down below our station. I recognize that old twisted cedar near the shore. It will be easier if we land there and leave the boat and walk the rest of the way home. It isn't very far."

In a moment, she had brought the boat in on the narrow sandy beach, and they all climbed out, thankful enough to stretch cramped limbs and realize they were so near home. They drew the boat well up and stamped her anchor in the sand and hid the oars in the bushes. But just as they were about to turn away and enter a path through the woods, Marty suddenly bent down and cried, pointing to something at her feet:

"Oh, look here! Do you see those footprints in the sand? They were made since last night because it was raining then, and I know whose they are!"

"Whose?" the other three questioned in chorus.

"They were made by *Chips Kilroy!*" declared Marty with great positiveness.

VIII

REVELATIONS BY MRS. GREENE

"BUT HOW DO YOU KNOW they were made by Chips Kilroy?" demanded Mr. Burnett. "Any boatman or crabber or some complete stranger might have landed here."

"Because they're special footprints," declared Marty. "Chips had something the matter with him when he was little—infantile paralysis, I think. It left him with something wrong with one foot. He sort of toes in with his left foot and limps a little. So it makes his right and left footprints different. You can see it here." She pointed down to a clear set where the boy had evidently stood a moment before moving on. The left print was somewhat shallower and decidedly "toed-in," as she had explained. So, the entire likelihood was that they had been made by Chips Kilroy.

"And here's another strange thing!" Marty went on. "He only got out of the boat and went away. There are no prints showing that he came back—and there's *no boat*! There's just a tiny mark of the prow of the boat left here. See it? The tide must have come and blotted out the rest. But what happened to the boat—and what's happened to him?"

"There might be several explanations to that," mused Mr. Burnett.

"Perhaps he was in a hurry and forgot to put out his anchor, and the incoming tide lifted the boat and carried it off. I've known *that* to happen. The offshore wind of this morning might easily have swept it clean away. There appears to be no anchor mark around that I can see. Or, another explanation might be that he was brought over in someone else's boat and landed here, and then the boat left. Perhaps they were supposed to come back for him later—or pick him up at some other spot."

"Maybe so," admitted Marty. "One thing is certain, though. He hasn't come back here—and he may still be around. Whatever he's come over for, I can't imagine. I hope he hasn't been bothering Nana. Anyway, his mother wasn't with him, or her footprints would have been here, too. I don't like it, somehow."

"Let's see where his footprints go," suggested Ted. "They seem to lead right along this path we're taking."

"Good idea. We'll keep them in sight as long as we can," agreed his father, "but I don't intend to follow them if they take us out of our way home. I'm chilly and wet, and so are all of you, and we can't get back to the house too quickly. Remember, I still have to go uptown to get the car before dark."

They plunged into the woods, Marty ahead, followed by Ted, and the others bringing up the rear. Ted was completely thrilled to be tracing Chips' footprints, still plainly visible in the sandy little path, packed fairly hard by the rain of the night before. The fog was thinner in the woods and did not interfere with their vision. But presently they emerged onto the rolling dunes, covered with seagrass, bayberry, and beach plum bushes, and thick with incoming fog from the nearby ocean. Somewhere on the more open trail they lost track of the footprints, much to Ted's disappointment. And at Mr. Burnett's command, they made straight for the lane and the warmth of the comfortable kitchen. They did not see a trace of the footprints again.

It was a rather distracted Mrs. Greene who admitted them to the coziness of the old kitchen, and a fully recovered Thusy also screeched a raucous welcome.

"I was some worried," Mrs. Greene admitted. "You be'n much later than you said—and this fog is bad! Thought you might have lost your way out on the bay. It's easy to do in this kind of weather."

They gave her an account of their adventures, and Marty finally demanded, "Have you seen Chips around here today, Nana? We saw tracks of where he had landed in the cove. I hope he wasn't here pestering you."

"Nary a sign of him," declared Mrs. Greene, "and I've been in the house all day. Cy was in for a little while, just setting round and talking, but 'cept for him, I haven't seen no one. If that Chips was over this side, he hasn't come near *this* place, or I'd have seen him. Heaven help him—if he tries to go back across the bay in *this* fog!"

It was all something of a mystery, but there was no way of unraveling it at this moment. After they'd changed to drier clothing, Mr. Burnett had to hurry away up to town on foot, to retrieve his car and unburden his mind to Captain Bell about his cranky little craft. Marty turned to and helped with the supper, and later Mr. Burnett came back, his slicker streaming with moisture, and announced that the wind had shifted northwest once more and that it was pouring rain.

The weather was certainly acting very perversely, but they dismissed it from their minds as they sat about the cozy supper table, consuming clam chowder, hot biscuits, rich creamed oysters, and blueberry pie. All were very jolly and very absorbed in recounting details of their visit to the South Inlet Station—all except Mrs. Greene. It was only Marty, however, who noticed that the old lady had a rather strained and anxious expression and said very little all through the meal.

"I wonder what Nana's worrying about," thought Marty. "It can't be because she thinks that Chips boy may be around. She doesn't care about *him*; it's the mother she doesn't like. I wonder if anything's happened today that she hasn't told us about." But Mrs. Greene vouchsafed no hint of what was on her mind during the meal, nor during the time when they all helped remove and wash the dishes and put them away.

Openly yawning and sleepy after their day outdoors, it was still too early to go to bed, and they sat about the warm kitchen. The two men were busy revamping some of their fishing tackle, Marty and Ted were idly teasing Thusy, and Mrs. Greene sat at the table, silently and rather grimly darning some stockings. Suddenly, to the amazement of them all, she laid the stocking on the table, straightened up, and announced:

"I got something to tell you all—and I might as well get it off my mind right away!" They all dropped what they were doing and stared at her in great bewilderment, but she went on doggedly:

"It's about this matter of Thusy and—and—Sailor Jack. I said too much last night when we were talking about them—or else not enough. I don't know how I got led into it; I've never told another soul, not even Marty. But there are some things I don't want you should misunderstand. I better tell you the whole thing—now!"

"Wait a moment, Mrs. Greene," interrupted Mr. Burnett gently. "Before you make any revelations you may not want to make, we must assure you that we haven't misunderstood anything, as you say, and would respect your silence if you prefer to keep it. We are, I must confess, deeply interested in this mystery about the macaw and the sailor, but we wouldn't for the world have you disclose anything you prefer personally not to reveal."

"That's kind of you to say so," went on the old lady, "but just the same, I think you'd better hear the rest. I'd feel better about it myself. You said a true word when you called it a mystery. It's more of a one than you know. When you keep a thing to yourself for years and years, it's sort of hard to speak about it. But since I've said what I did last night, I'd better go on and tell the whole thing. You're all so kind—I sort of feel like you was my own family!" She took off her glasses, wiped them nervously, and set them back.

It seemed very hard for her to begin. Thinking to help her out, Mr. Burnett ventured, "You may be sure that anything you see fit to tell us, Mrs. Greene, will be kept in absolute confidence."

"I know that," she returned, "or I wouldn't be telling it! The thing's been pestering me for years! Well, it was this way. I told you last night—or you found out from the record book—how Thusy and Sailor Jack come ashore that terrible night. He told us afterwards that he'd never have been saved either, only when they first run on the sandbar, he knew that the worst had happened, and he run right down to his cabin to get Thusy and his canvas bag of belongings. He put Thusy in the bag, too, and then run back on deck. There'd been eight men and the captain there when he left. When he come back, there was nary a soul on board—and he knew what'd happened. A big wave had struck the ship and swept 'em all off. If he hadn't been below, he'd have gone, too!

"He was the only one there to catch the breeches-buoy line when it come over. Three times it fell too short, but he caught the last one. Then, when he was getting into the buoy, a big spar fell off the mast right on his leg and broke it. He said he never did know how he managed to climb in, with the pain of it, but he did, and they pulled him ashore. He said his mind was kind of blank after that for a while—what with his leg and the shock and all. Captain Kilroy kept him there at the station for nigh a week, in the Distress Room, and they couldn't get a doctor from the mainland 'cause the weather was so terrible. I told you all that last night—and how Abner, my husband, finally took him in here, and how he lived here the rest of his days. But there's a lot more to it than that—"

Again she fumbled nervously with her spectacles and took up the stocking she had been mending.

"I'd better go on with this darning while I talk," she explained. "Keeps me from getting fidgety if I do something with my hands!" They were all listening now, with breathless attention, and she went on more calmly after a moment.

"I told you last night how Sailor Jack seemed to have plenty of money—at least, he had all he needed. He never seemed to spend it too freely, but when he wanted something, he got it. He seemed to be an educated man, talked good English and knew several other languages—so he said. He liked to read the papers and books. He used to send for books from the city, and he got quite a library of 'em after a while. I have 'em yet—up in that room he used to have. They're mostly all about history and foreign lands and things like that. He used to talk quite a bit about his travels, strange places he'd been. But he never said a living word about himself—or his family—or how he came to be a common sailor traveling around on ordinary ships. Not once did he ever mention *that*, and, of course, we never asked him. That was *his* business, and it didn't concern us! But we both got very fond of him. After a while he seemed just like one of the family. And he was certainly crazy about that bird, Methuselah. He named him that himself, he told us, out of the Bible, 'cause he said the bird was fairly old, even when *he* got him."

"Where did he get Thusy, I wonder, and how long had he had him? Did he ever tell you?" questioned Mr. Burnett at this point.

"Oh, yes, he told us all about that," continued Mrs. Greene. "He said he got him somewhere in South America—bought him from a native there who had him for sale on the street because the bird talked pretty. And he'd kept him ever since because Thusy seemed like company for him, someone he could talk to when he was so much by himself. Sailor Jack was handy with tools, too. He made that perch for Thusy and used to take it and the bird around with him outside, when he sat there over to the barn when he used to saw wood for us sometimes, even up to his room with him at night. He used to talk to Thusy a lot in French and teach him to say things in that language, too. Thusy could talk French quite nice then, but it's so many years ago that he's forgotten most of it now. Sailor Jack did tell us he was French himself, and it made him feel sort of at home to have Thusy speak it. But that's all he ever did tell us about himself."

"How long was he with you?" asked Mr. Burnett.

"Must have been about fourteen years or more," said Mrs. Greene. "About a year before he died, he was awful sick one time, something wrong with his heart. My husband and I nursed him through it. He was so bad for a while that we thought he was going to die right then—and so did he. One day he said to us:

"'I have a lot to be grateful to the both of you for. I think I'm going to die, but I want you to have Methuselah to keep as long as he lives. And there's a black box. I have it hidden. There is a letter in it that will tell you something—' And then he sort of became unconscious and didn't speak again for a long time. When he was getting better, we thought he'd say something more about it—but he never did! And, of course, we didn't like to remind him about it. And, do you know, when he *did* die all of a sudden-like, about a year later, he'd never said a thing about that black box! We hunted for it high and low, my husband and I, but never a trace of it did we find. We were sure it must be somewhere about the place, but it never turned up. I'm certain he meant to tell us sometime, only he didn't think he was going to pass away so soon. Just sitting on a chair, he was—right in this kitchen, reading the paper—and suddenly he keeled right over and was gone. I've always figured he thought he'd probably have another long sickness before his end, and he'd tell us then. He didn't never dream he'd go so quick. But ever since, off and on, I've hunted the place over for that black box. And there ain't an inch of this house I haven't searched—but nary a sign of it have I ever found. That's the mystery I told you there was about him!"

She was silent suddenly and sat back with a deep sigh, as if feeling immense relief at having at last made this revelation. The others had been leaning forward in their chairs in intense interest. Marty, amazed herself at the curious story, noticed that Ted's eyes were sparkling with excitement, his hands clutched together till the knuckles showed white.

"Then—there's a *treasure*, Mrs. Greene! There *must* be! And it's hidden somewhere in a black box! Oh, couldn't we help you hunt for it? It would be wonderful if it could be found!"

His father laughed at his excitement and admitted that all of them would like nothing better than to engage in this treasure hunt. But he went on more soberly:

"This is a rather amazing story you have told us, Mrs. Greene. But it also seems to me to have a number of angles that we haven't gone into. May I ask a few more questions?"

"Ask away!" smiled Mrs. Greene, now going on with her mending in a calmer frame of mind. "I've told you what was most on my mind—how Sailor Jack come to be here and how he died and how we never could find that box. I didn't want that you should misunderstand about all this. What else may it be that you want to know?"

"Well," he hesitated, "I'll have to confess that I've been doing some more studying of those record books at the station, and this morning I came across an item or two that seemed rather singular." And he explained to her, in full, his curious discovery about the affairs of Keeper Kilroy.

"Forgive me if I'm mistaken," he went on, "but it seems as if this Kilroy affair might in some way be involved with the matter of Sailor Jack and Thusy—and your husband, the following keeper. It has seemed strange to me that, after all these years, his descendants should still be making themselves a nuisance to you, unless they thought they still had some hold on you. Let me read you a paragraph or two from a letter I had from Professor Sedgwick this morning that may explain what I mean."

Mrs. Greene listened rather tight-lipped while he read to her what Marty had heard him read that same morning in the boat.

"You see," he ended, "this remark of Mrs. Kilroy's about 'a good time to look' must have meant that she, too, felt there was something concealed—probably this same black box. But my wonder is how she came to know of it—or, even if she did, what right she would have to seek for it, no doubt with the intention of taking it from you. But if it distresses you to answer this, Mrs. Greene, I beg of you not to do so!"

"I don't mind the least bit," answered Mrs. Greene, rather grimly. "That's another thing's been pestering me for some years. So's you can understand it, I have to go back and explain about Alvin

Kilroy—and what kind of a keeper he was. He'd been a good coast guard in the beginning, had entered the service as soon as he was old enough. And he'd been keeper a good many years. But toward the end, he began to get awful careless. Abner said it was terrible the things he neglected and the way he let things go. Abner was 'number one man' under him, and he had to cover up the greatest lot of mistakes and write up the record book most of the time. They was all kind of fond of old Kilroy—he'd been there so long—and they figured he must have something the matter with him, some kind of disease coming on, or something, that made him so sleepy and indifferent all the time. He didn't drink, so it wasn't that. But he acted sort of like it a good deal of the time, as if he wasn't all there. It wasn't quite time for him to retire, and the rest of the crew sort of kept carrying him along and covering up his mistakes till that time come. But it was awful hard on Abner sometimes, 'specially when the old man got into some real trouble."

The old lady's eyes looked misty with remembered troubles as she wove her darning needle in and out of the stocking, and she was silent a moment, evidently thinking how to continue. Presently she resumed:

"Once in a while he'd stay plumb in his bed when there was a wreck going on and leave Abner to take charge of it all. Or he'd go out with the crew and give wrong orders and risk the lives of his men without any need. That's what happened just before he got dismissed. There was a terrible bad storm one night, and a ship come in on the bar and signaled for help. It was a good piece down the beach, and instead of sending down the cart and rigging up the breeches buoy, he sent six men out in the lifeboat—and Abner was one of them. Abner knew no lifeboat could last five minutes in a sea like that—much less get to the wreck—but he had to go. Kilroy insisted on it. They did manage to get her out, but all of a sudden she capsized. Abner and three of the men just managed to get to shore alive—but two of 'em was drowned.

"Kilroy had to answer for that. There was an investigation, and the superintendent sent for Abner, and he had to go and testify what the state of affairs was—and he had to tell the truth. He'd had to take his oath he would. He hated to do it against the old man, but there wasn't no other way. They dismissed Kilroy from the station as keeper. They'd have dismissed him from the service, too, if it hadn't been Abner pleaded with them not to dismiss him entirely. So they lowered his rank and sent him to another station to be a number five man. Kilroy took it awful hard and blamed Abner for it all, 'specially after Abner got put in his place. He lived long enough after it to retire, but he only got a pension based on his number five rating and not what he'd have got as keeper. But his family's had it in for us ever since, 'specially that daughter-in-law. She comes over and heckles the life out of me, year in and year out, as if I was responsible!"

Mrs. Greene sighed, rolled up a pair of stockings she'd finished darning, and picked up a fresh one from her basket. Her audience, still listening intently, stirred in their chairs uneasily and waited for her to continue. But she was silent, her mind probably occupied with the memories of those former years. Outside, the rain seemed to be beating down with vicious intensity, and a driving wind rattled the old window shutters and casements. But no one paid it any heed.

Suddenly Ted could contain himself no longer and burst out, "But, Mrs. Greene, would you mind telling us how Thusy and Sailor Jack came to be mixed up with it all? Is—is there something else?"

The old lady came back to the present with a start and smiled rather grimly. "Yes—there is!" she declared. "I just kind of got thinking about the past and forgot to go on. I was going to tell you how—"

She never finished the sentence, for at that instant there came a startling crash that froze the words on her lips and stunned them all with sudden shock.

IX

INTRUDER IN THE NIGHT

MARTY ALWAYS REMEMBERED AFTERWARD THE strange expression on all their faces at the sound of that crash. Startled astonishment mainly, frozen immobility for an instant, mingling with just a little fear in that of her grandmother. The spell was broken the next moment, for the sound had wakened Thusy from a nap, and his immediate raucous squawking was hideous to hear. "Stop that, Thusy!" she cried, and followed it with the question, "What on earth was *that*?"

"It came from the pantry," declared Mrs. Greene. "Mebbe it was only the wind knocking something over." They all made a dash for the dark little pantry whose door opened into the kitchen. Ted pulled a small flashlight from his pocket, and in this illumination, they saw that an empty milk bottle, which had been standing on the ledge of the small high window, had fallen to the floor and smashed into several pieces. The window was open, as it was on a side away from the heavy rain and was protected only by a rusty screen.

"Couldn't have been the wind that blew it over," declared Mrs. Greene. "Look at *that*!" She pointed to the screen, which exhibited a large hole directly in its center. "That wasn't there before!"

"Somebody's been around here!" exclaimed Mr. Burnett. "But how they could have got at that screen beats me! Taking in the foundations of the house outside, that window is more than ten feet from the ground. I'll get my big flashlight and go outside and see what's happened. The rest of you had better stay indoors. The rain is coming down in torrents." He rushed upstairs to get his torch and came down in his slicker and sou'wester, only to find that all had wrapped themselves in some protection against the weather and were insisting on accompanying him outside. Thusy, meanwhile, continued squawking vociferously, adding to the confusion.

"Don't get excited!—Don't get excited!—" he shrieked quite aptly. But no one paid him any further attention. In another moment they were all out in the driving rain, scurrying around the corner of the house to survey the ground below the pantry window. Their flashlights turned the drenching rain to streamers of silver and illuminated a strange state of affairs.

For, below the window, an old wooden bench and a couple of discarded wooden chicken coops were lying helter-skelter, and it took no great amount of imagining to realize what had happened. Someone had been standing on them, piled up so that the window would be within reach, and the rickety edifice had suddenly collapsed, no doubt to the great discomfort of the intruder.

"I think I can imagine what happened," speculated Mr. Burnett. "Someone has been prowling about here, with what intention we don't know, but I'm pretty sure that person was trying to listen at that open window to our conversation in the kitchen. It must have been quite audible with the pantry door open. In order to reach the window and hear better, he had piled up the bench and boxes, but the affair must have been pretty unsteady. Some movement he made must have sent the thing toppling. Maybe he grabbed at the window to save himself, punching the hole through the screen and knocking over the milk bottle inside. But where is the intruder now? That is the question! I should have thought the fall might have injured him quite a bit, but he seems to have gotten away."

"Let's hunt for footprints!" cried Ted, no doubt thinking of their experience of the afternoon. There were trampled footprints around the scene under the window, they saw, as they turned the flashlights downward. But they were so confused and washed out by the heavy rain that nothing could be made of them. Widening the circle of light, they discovered that these led off in the darkness in the general direction of the old barn, at some distance from the house. The rain had made these equally indistinct, but their direction was apparent.

"He's made for the barn, looks like!" declared Mrs. Greene. "But if you folks want to follow 'em, I'm going back into the house. Don't like to leave it alone. He might come back, whoever 'tis!" she ended cannily.

"Well, you just give a loud yell if anything happens there that bothers you," agreed Mr. Burnett, "and we'll all come running!"

He and his party disappeared through the rain and the darkness, and Mrs. Greene turned back into the kitchen, where the parrot promptly announced, "Thusy's very—very hungry!" Crossly telling him to go back to sleep (which he promptly did!), she sat down to await their return and, meanwhile, finished the stocking she had been mending when the fracas began. The intrusion had certainly disturbed her, but she was not one to let such things interfere with her daily tasks. Presently, they all came trooping back.

"No sign of him!" announced Marty, discarding her raincoat.

"But we know who it is!" supplemented Ted, his cheeks red with excitement, his dark curls streaming with rain. "We found a couple of footprints that hadn't all been washed out by the rain. They were under some bushes. They're Chips' prints; we're sure of that!"

"*Chips?*" cried Mrs. Greene. "But he should be over t'other side of the bay—long ago. What's he doing around here this time of night—and out in such a terrible storm?"

"That's what I'd like to know!" echoed Marty indignantly. "I knew he wasn't over here for any good—this afternoon when we saw his tracks. But I thought he'd get home somehow, even if he had to walk or hitchhike. He must have been listening to all you were telling us, Nana. I wonder why?"

"But where did he *go*?" demanded Mrs. Greene, thinking on another line. "Did you look for him in the barn?"

"We scoured the whole place," put in Mr. Burnett. "We lost the tracks in the grass and shrubbery before we came to the barn, but we hunted the whole place over anyhow. I rather think he wouldn't try the barn because we'd be likely to think he might have taken refuge there. Wherever he is on this stormy night, I feel rather sorry for him out in it. But I must say, I don't like the idea of his prowling around here. From what you have told me, I don't think he intends any harm, but I can't imagine why he should be spying on us. There's something back of all this, something we don't understand!"

Singularly enough, it was Marty who came to the defense of Chips. "No, Chips *isn't* a bad boy—really," she declared vehemently. "It's just that nobody seems to understand him. I'm awfully sorry for him because nobody likes him, hardly ever says a kind word to him. And his mother nearly drives him crazy trying to get him to do things he doesn't want to do. He's real clever in some ways, too, but nobody seems to have found it out yet. But I still don't see what he's doing over here at night—and in such a dreadful storm!"

"What do you think we ought to do about it, Mrs. Greene?" inquired Mr. Burnett anxiously. "I don't like the idea of his prowling about, and I don't like to think of his having no place of shelter this stormy night either. Shall I go over and get Captain Cy and try to hunt him up? Together, we might be able to round him up somehow."

But Mrs. Greene shook her head. "No need to get fussed about him not having shelter," she declared. "He'll find that somewheres. And I don't think he'll bother with this place again tonight, either. He's had too good a scare! I think we better all go to bed and forget it."

But the others were too excited to go to bed just then, and Ted demanded imploringly, "We *can't* go till you've told us the rest of that story, Mrs. Greene. You were just going to when that crash came. Won't you finish it now?"

"Ah, yes! Zee end of eet," echoed Monsieur. "I cannot sleep eef I do not hear zis so interesting tale!"

Marty and Mr. Burnett were equally anxious to hear it, so Mrs. Greene patiently seated herself once more and took up another stocking from what seemed a never-ending heap in the darning basket. Threading a needle close to her nose, she went on:

"Well, let's see . . . where was I? Oh, I remember now. I was just going to tell you about what happened between Sailor Jack and Captain Kilroy. It's a strange thing—that part of it! I never knew the right of it till Sailor Jack told us, a long time afterward. Seems that when Sailor Jack was first rescued and was so sick at the station, some pretty curious things went on. His leg was so bad and his pain so awful, he says he must have been out of his head some of the time. Probably said a lot of things when he was that way that he didn't remember afterwards.

"Old Kilroy tried to do what he could for him at first, but he soon got tired of that and left most of the job to Abner. Kilroy used to sit by Jack quite a lot, though, and listen to what he was babbling when he was kind of out of his head. I never did know what he heard, but something happened one night that put an end to *that*! Sailor Jack told me about it long afterwards.

"Seems Jack was lying there sort of half asleep. He wasn't out of his head then, but Kilroy must have thought he was unconscious or deep asleep because Jack suddenly realized that something odd was going on. I told you how he had all his belongings in a canvas bag, and he'd insisted on keeping that bag right near his bed. But this night he opened his eyes and seen old Kilroy over t'other side of the room near the lamp. He had Jack's bag by him and was going over everything in it. Just as Jack looked at him, he had this black box in his hand and was shaking it and trying to get it open.

"Jack told us he knew right then and there that this had to stop, but he didn't want to offend the keeper who'd given him shelter.

Instead of calling out or anything like that, Jack began to groan and toss as if he was in great pain, but keeping his eyes shut all the while. It gave old Kilroy quite a scare, and he shoved things into the canvas bag again and kicked it behind a chair. Then he came across the room to take a look at Jack. Jack told me he kept the keeper running all night, waiting on him, and him pretending he was a lot worse than he was. Didn't give Kilroy another chance to look over the bag. And by and by it was time for Abner to come on duty, and Kilroy had to go to bed.

"When he had Abner to himself, Jack told him he wanted to be taken away from the station as soon as possible, and where could he go? Abner said there wasn't no place but his own house, right nearby, but he'd be glad to take him in there, as it wasn't no place for a sick man in the station anyhow. Jack begged Abner to take him away the very next day and said he'd pay him well for his trouble. Abner said he mustn't consider that, but he would speak to Kilroy the next day about having him removed at once.

"Kilroy didn't like the plan—and good reason he had! But there wasn't much he could argue about it, so they brought Sailor Jack here the very next day. And I've told you how he stayed on after that. But this wasn't the end of it, as far as Kilroy was concerned. I used to notice after Jack was around and well again that Kilroy often come over here to talk to him—never in the house but always outside where I couldn't hear what was said. I noticed, besides, that Jack was always very peevish and upset after one of these talks. Once I asked him what Kilroy was bothering him about. Jack was real mad that time, but all he would say was that Kilroy wanted to know whether he was going to keep his promise. When I asked what that promise was, Jack only said, 'Never you mind! It must have been something I said when I was out of my head, but it doesn't mean anything!'

"Then Kilroy had that trouble and got dismissed from the station, and we didn't see him anymore. And about a year later, he died, and that seemed to be the end of it. We all lived quite peaceful after that, and then Sailor Jack died himself about 1914. And about a year after that, Abner passed on, too, and I was left all alone for quite a while. It wasn't till about eight years ago that this here Kilroy woman turned up one day. She is old Kilroy's widow, and I couldn't believe my ears when she began heckling me about a fortune or a lot of money—or something like that—that she said we'd got away from Sailor Jack and that rightly belonged to her father-in-law, old Alvin Kilroy!

"I told her she was crazy, that Sailor Jack hadn't left us nothing but the parrot. Far as we knew, he didn't have nothing to leave! Then she up and said even the parrot didn't rightly belong to me, because Sailor Jack had promised him, and a lot of money besides, to Kilroy when he was lying so sick in the Distress Room. He'd given a solemn promise that Kilroy could have it all when he died. So I was to hand it all over, or she'd have the law on me. I told her to go ahead and have it, 'twouldn't do her much good. I didn't have nothing of Sailor Jack's but Thusy, and he'd said a hundred times that Thusy was to be ours if he should pass on. And I said, what's more, I didn't believe Jack had given Kilroy any promise that time. He was delirious pretty near the whole time he was there, so it didn't matter much *what* he said.

"She claimed a promise was a promise, no matter how it was given, and she was going to have her rights. I didn't see what rights *she* would have had in it, even if there'd been anything, and I said so. Well, to make a long story short, that's been about the way of it ever since. Every so often she comes over here, putting in her claim, till nowadays I won't even let her in—if I see her first! What makes me maddest is to think she came over here that one time when I wasn't home and was planning to go snooping around, trying to find something! I've never left the house alone and unlocked since then.

"I guess I've told you everything now!" Mrs. Greene ended with a sigh. Putting down the stocking, she rose and went over to the range to give it a shaking down for the night. The others drew a long sigh of relaxed tension, and Mr. Burnett was just about to make some comment when Mrs. Greene suddenly straightened up from bending in front of the range and faced them with a shocked expression.

"How—how long do you s'pose that Chips Kilroy was listening at the pantry window?" she demanded a little breathlessly.

"We can't tell," admitted Mr. Burnett. "For all we know, he may have been there all the evening. Why?"

"Then," cried Mrs. Greene in great distress, "he probably heard what I told you about the *black box*! I never told his mother anything about *that*!"

X

MORNING ADVENTURE

Far into the night Marty awoke, roused to intense awareness by something, the origin of which she could not for a moment identify.

They had all gone to bed very late that night. After Mrs. Greene's horrified announcement, they had sat about the kitchen discussing the possibilities of what Chips might have overheard, in all their various phases. What he might have been there for to begin with, they could not quite fathom. Mr. Burnett had suggested that he might have been prevented from getting back across the bay by the fog and was perhaps trying to find a place to stay overnight. But in that case, it had seemed that he should have come openly to the door and disclosed his predicament. To have been eavesdropping in that fashion at a window seemed, indeed, a little more sinister. They could find no answer to the problem, nor that of how much he might have overheard. The fact that he must still be in the vicinity also disturbed them all. But when Mr. Burnett had discovered, in glancing at the clock, that it was nearly midnight, with common consent, they all departed for bed.

"Try not to think about it anymore tonight," Mr. Burnett had advised. "Tomorrow, in daylight, we'll try to get to the bottom of this mystery!"

That had been all very well, but, nevertheless, Marty had remained long awake, mulling over the problem, and she rather guessed that the others had not found it any too easy to get to sleep either. However, she had dropped off at last, to sleep deeply and dreamlessly, till a sudden awakening by some sound not yet located. The rain was still sluicing down and the wind blowing hard. She had just concluded that it must probably have been the banging of a loose shutter that had awakened her when the sound came again—a soft rapping at her door!

Hastily jumping out of bed, she threw on a wrapper and found the door in the dark, wondering wildly who could be rousing her at this hour—and for what reason. Opening the door a crack, she whispered, "Who is it? What is the matter?"

"It's only I—Ted!" came back another whisper. "I—I couldn't get to sleep—and I've been hearing a strange sound—somewhere under my window. I didn't want to tell Dad because he'd worry about my not sleeping—and so would Monsieur—so I came to you. Will you come in my room and listen? Maybe we can find out what's going on."

Marty was instantly all agog. "Wait till I light a candle," she breathed.

"No, don't light one," warned Ted. "If it's someone outside, they might see it and get away! Then we'd never know who it was!"

Marty agreed that this idea was the best, and together they tiptoed softly down the long passageway and into Ted's room where, groping their way around the furniture, he led her to the open window facing south and therefore sheltered from the slashing northeast rain. It opened on the same side as the pantry window below and was only a few feet to the left of it. Without a word, they crouched by the window, staring out into the rain and darkness, which was so dense that absolutely nothing could be discerned below. And for the moment, only the sounds of drenching rain and grinding, creaking tree branches were audible.

Marty had just begun to think that Ted, in his unwonted excitement, must have imagined it all, when something else happened! There came the sound of a muffled *thud*, as if someone had dropped heavily to the ground, followed by the rustle of bushes or shrubbery close by.

"I'll bet that's Chips again!" breathed Marty. "And it sounds as if he got in this time—and then got out again! I'll give him the scare of his life!" And she shouted, "*Hi!*" into the darkness outside. The effect was immediate, for the noise of footfalls and crashing through the underbrush came to them plainly, till it died away in the rain and darkness.

Curiously enough, the noise of Marty's shout had disturbed no one else in the sleeping household, though she had fully expected everyone would be instantly aroused by it. As she and Ted listened, there was not a sound of anyone moving, so the two consulted as to what ought to be done next.

"We'd better go down and see what's happened in the pantry," decided Marty. "No use waking the others just yet, until we see what he was there for. Light your candle, Ted, and we'll go down—unless you'd rather stay here."

"I'm going, too!" declared Ted stoutly. "Do you—do you suppose he's stolen Thusy?"

"Not unless Chips chloroformed him first. The racket would be terrible!" chuckled Marty, as Ted groped about, found the candle and matches on his little bedside table, and struck a light. Still with the slumbering household undisturbed, they tiptoed down the stairs, through the lower hall, and into the kitchen.

"Where's Thusy?" gasped Ted, looking about and noting at once that the place where his perch always stood was vacant.

"Don't worry!" grinned Marty. "Nana always takes Thusy to her room when she goes to bed at night. She's never trusted him alone here in the kitchen at night as long as I can remember."

"Well, maybe he didn't get Thusy, but I'm certain that's what he was after!" announced Ted with great positiveness.

"Perhaps that's so," agreed Marty. "But now let's look in the pantry." They turned their steps in that direction and stood in the doorway, holding the candle high. To all appearances, nothing there was disturbed. Even the little window was closed and the wooden outside shutter hooked, as Marty remembered that it had been left the night before by her grandmother. Whatever the intruder had been after, there was no evidence of his having been in that particular room. The two stared at each other in some amazement.

"He couldn't have been here!" whispered Ted. "Where do you suppose he got out, then?"

"Let's look around the kitchen," decided Marty. And they turned back to stare about the larger room. It speedily became evident, in that swift inspection, what had really happened. A larger window in that room, facing in the same direction as the one in the pantry, stood wide open to the rain and darkness!

"Look!" cried Ted. "*There's* where he got in—and out!"

What had happened was all too evident. Mrs. Greene had taken out the folding screen the night before and closed and locked it while they were still at supper, as the slight draft and dampness from it had been directly at Ted's back. It had remained so all during the evening and when they had all retired. But one of the panes in it, near the lock, had long been cracked and rather loose, and could easily have been removed by someone outside and the lock unfastened. Also the window was much nearer the ground than the high pantry one and would not require the high edifice of bench and chicken coops. This the intruder must have discovered earlier in the evening—and availed himself of it later when all the household was safely in bed.

"But why did he get in? What was he after?" demanded Marty impatiently. "Nothing seems to have been disturbed. He got out that window and ran off—that's the thud we heard, when he landed. But what was he *doing* in here?"

"I must have heard him when he was first trying to get in," commented Ted. "Must have been when he was taking out that pane of glass. It was a strange sort of noise it made. I couldn't think what it was. Then I heard another scraping sound—that must have been when he was raising the window. And right after that, I came to call you. So he couldn't have been in here long!"

"I wonder what we ought to do?" queried Marty, glancing at the kitchen clock. "It's only a little after four—not nearly light yet—and I sort of hate to wake the others since we got to sleep so late. And yet, with Chips still prowling around, I don't feel comfortable going back to bed. I'm not a bit sleepy anymore, after all this excitement. Tell you what—you go back to bed, Ted, and I'll light the lamp and sit here and read till daylight. Chips won't try it again anyhow. We've scared him off twice. But I'm not taking any chances!"

"I'd rather stay down here, too," declared Ted. "I just can't go back to bed and sleep, and I hate lying awake in the dark, listening for things. Let's both stay down here and—"

Suddenly both of them were startled almost out of their bedroom slippers by a stealthy sound out in the hall—so startled that Marty almost dropped the candle she was holding! They whirled instantly to face the door and there beheld a curious sight. It was Monsieur, his form enveloped in a great woolly bathrobe, his white hair tousled till it stood on end, and with a large flashlight in his hand that he had turned on them in a white glare.

"Vat ees all zis?" he demanded wonderingly. "My door, eet stands partly open at zee head of zee stairs—I wake and I hear zee strange sounds from zee kitchen—zee whispering—zee moving around! Me, I sink someone get een here once more. And zen I come softly down—and I see *you!* Ees anysing wrong?"

As rapidly as possible, they explained to him the curious situation that had arisen while he ran his free hand through his already wildly distorted hair. And at the end, he muttered his own ultimatum:

"Me—*I* stay down here zee rest of zis night! I do not sleep again—nevaire—when once I wake in zee night. So I stay here and make some notes on my music zat I have long neglect. Ted and

Marty, you go back and get zee sleep you need. Een zee morning, we find out more about zis strange affair!"

He was firm in his decision, nor could they budge him from it. So Marty lighted the lamp, and the two left him to his vigil. And shortly thereafter, in their relief that someone else was keeping watch, they had both fallen fast asleep, not to waken till Mrs. Greene rang a loud rising bell at the foot of the stairs, half an hour before breakfast.

It was all explained at the breakfast table next morning to Mr. Burnett, who had arrived last, still yawning and sleepy after his late retiring, but who had slept through everything till the bell rang. Mrs. Greene already knew the history of the night from Monsieur, whom she had found, to her great astonishment, fast asleep with his head on his arms on the kitchen table. Her astonishment had been great, and it increased considerably when Monsieur had explained the situation. She had come into the kitchen carrying Thusy on his perch, who had straightway greeted the sight of the sleeping Frenchman with a raucous screeching.

"Well, zat Thusy, he ees at least still here," Monsieur had sighed in relief at the sight of him, and then he had explained. When they were all assembled at breakfast, Mr. Burnett also had to be enlightened. He shook his head ruefully over having slept soundly through all the excitement and later remarked:

"I wonder if it's possible that Chips may really have been after Thusy? He may have planned to carry him off somehow, late in the night, when he thought we were all deeply asleep and, not finding him in the kitchen as he had expected, departed empty handed."

"That's what I've been thinking right along!" agreed Ted, and the others solemnly nodded.

But Mrs. Greene chuckled, "He didn't depart so empty handed after all—as I found out when I started to get breakfast! There's a half a leg of cold lamb missing out of the icebox and part of a loaf of bread. And, by the way, did anyone of you leave forty-five cents on top of the icebox yesterday?"

No one had, and they said so positively, wondering why she asked such a curious question.

"Well, I found it there this morning," she went on, "and I didn't leave it there myself. Where it come from, I can't think."

"I know!" cried Marty suddenly. "That explains it. It was *Chips*! He was probably hungry and took the food, but he's *honest*, I know that—and he left some money there to help pay for it. That's what he wanted, not Thusy! He could pay something for the food, but he never could pay for Thusy, and he wouldn't take what doesn't belong to him."

"But don't forget," warned Mr. Burnett, "that he may think Thusy really belongs to them. Remember that his mother does!" That thought had its disquieting aspects, they all had to agree.

"But what are we going to do now?" demanded Ted as they finished breakfast and rose from the table.

"I know what I'm going to do," said Mr. Burnett decidedly. "I'm going to get my boots and slicker on and walk up to town to get the mail. I have some very important business letters coming in today, and I must have them without delay. I shan't take the car. It's still pouring and blowing hard, and that land out toward the beach is a running river. I'd never get the car through it. But I'll do any errands you wish, Mrs. Greene, while I'm in town. The rest of you had better stay indoors. It's pretty vile weather—and liable to keep up all day."

"Too bad you have to have such a storm right in the middle of your business vacation," mourned Mrs. Greene. "It's a regular four-day northeaster. I've known 'em to keep it up a solid week—but not often."

"We, too, we take zee morning off, Ted," added Monsieur. "Zose pianos, zey get so out of zee tune zis damp day, we could not use zem. I have to tune zem once again before we do. Me, I lose zee sleep last night, and I feel—vat you call—no good! I go to lie down on my bed zis morning to take zee leetle extra nap."

Presently Mr. Burnett had departed on his errand, Monsieur

had gone to his room, Marty was helping Mrs. Greene with the kitchen work, and Ted, after having made his bed, was roaming disconsolately about. For a while, he tried coaxing Thusy to talk, but the macaw was also feeling the depressing effects of the weather and would only advise him crossly to "Go fly a kite!" After which, he tucked his head under his wing and pretended to go to sleep. When Marty had at last finished her work, Ted came to her with a proposition of his own.

"Let's you and I get on boots and slickers, Marty," he suggested, "and go out to the barn and see whether we can find any traces of Chips. I'm sure he must have spent the night there. It's about the only shelter he'd have out of the rain. He might even be there now! Anyway, we might be able to find out what he's been doing and possibly where he's gone."

Marty was enthusiastically agreeable, and they went to get on suitable clothes for the drenching trip. Mrs. Greene watched them go, admonishing them not to stay out too long and directing Marty to look for any eggs that one of her stray hens might have laid there. And, in a complete outfit of boots, slickers, and sou'westers, they sloshed through the yard, which was by now an actual shallow lake, toward the old barn, their heads bent against the driving wind that almost knocked them off their feet.

"Suppose we find Chips out there?" shouted Ted as he splashed along at Marty's side. "What'll we do?"

"No fear!" she shouted back. "I don't think he'd dare to stay there in the daytime—with so many of us around!"

The barn was some two hundred feet from the house, a picturesque old building in a very decided state of disrepair. Marty explained that when her grandfather had been alive, he had kept a horse or two and some farming vehicles, such as a horse-drawn plow, and that he had done considerable farming about the place before he died, but that since then, her grandmother had disposed of the horses and given up any farming except for their small garden of vegetables. So the barn had been left to fall into disuse, only the chickens occasionally inhabiting it.

The big main doors were shut and locked, but they entered through the smaller door of an old feed and harness room. The damp, musty smell of ancient hay greeted them as they stood staring about the small space given over to feed boxes, long empty, and mildewed harness still hanging about on pegs from the wall. The one small window was partly broken and so dirty and cobwebby that very little daylight could struggle through. As they started about, searching for traces of Chips, Ted suddenly spied great, wet footprints on the wooden floor and pointed them out excitedly.

"See? He was here!" he cried. "Those are his prints, same as we saw in the sand. Let's look in the other part—quick!"

They entered the main part of the barn through a door opening from the feed room. This enclosure, a large one, was very dim as it was lighted only by one small window up near the roof. At one side were two stalls for horses, with their mangers. In the center bulked an old hay cart, and various rusty farm tools stood about the walls. Over the stalls was a high loft where hay had once been stored, and a long ladder resting against it provided means of reaching it. There was no sign of Chips in the main part of the barn, and the leaky roof was admitting streams of rainwater where old shingles had long been missing.

"Let's try the hayloft," whispered Marty. "It's the only place where we haven't looked." Ted started scrambling up the ladder, and she followed, warning him to be careful of insecure rungs. But there was no Chips in the loft either. However, signs of his having been there were soon apparent. An armful or two of very musty and ancient hay had been piled in a corner where there was no leakage, and over it had been thrown an old and very moth-eaten horse blanket.

"Look at that!" cried Marty. "That must've been where he slept. Nana always keeps that blanket down in the feed room to put over chicken coops when she has some young chicks. He must have carried it up here. And you can see he must have slept on that pile of hay. Look at the dent he made in the middle of it! But where is he now?"

They stared about them a moment, in silence broken only by the drumming rain on the leaky roof. Then they descended to the ground and wandered back to the feed room. Suddenly Ted, who had been roaming about, idly lifting the lids of the feed bins, called out, "Oh, see *here*!"

Marty rushed over and peered down where he pointed and then burst into a hearty chuckle. For, resting on an old newspaper, they beheld the half-demolished leg of cold lamb and the part of a bread loaf that Mrs. Greene had missed that very morning.

"That can only mean one thing," she surmised. "Chips must be coming back. He'd have taken them with him when he left, if he hadn't been. Maybe he doesn't dare stay around the barn in the daytime, for fear he'll be seen, but is planning to sleep here again tonight. Now, I wonder, what for?"

"To get Thusy this time!" declared Ted. "He missed out on it last night, and maybe he's going to find out what room Mrs. Greene keeps him in and come back tonight for another try." It did seem highly possible, if that were Chips' intention.

"I don't see quite how he'd dare try it again," mused Marty, "and yet, it's quite likely he thinks we don't know who last night's intruder *was*. He most likely doesn't realize we recognized his footprints. He probably figures we thought it was just some stranger or tramp who got scared off and wouldn't come back again."

"I'd like to know where he is now!" said Ted. "He can't have gone so very far away in such a storm. Tell you what, Marty, let's try to follow him up. We haven't anything else to do, and we're dressed so the storm won't hurt us. Let's see if we can't find his footprints around and trace him. We might discover something; who knows!"

It seemed a reasonable idea. There was really nothing much else they could do on this stormy morning, and their quest might result in something more definite concerning their mystery. Opening the feed room door, they stepped out into a fierce deluge of rain and an ever-increasing wind. The force of it almost took them off their feet at first, before they braced themselves to meet it.

"Ted," cried Marty, "this storm is *awful*! I think maybe we'd better go back to the house after all." But Ted had found a trace of footsteps which, though rapidly disappearing, led with distinctness from the door down the path in the direction of the bay.

"Oh, never mind the rain!" he cried impatiently. "Here's the way he went. Let's follow it up!" Marty herself gave in then, lured by a curiosity too strong to be withstood.

And so, with the wind at their backs helping them along, the two disappeared down the winding path between the heavy growth of cedars, following the trail of Chips Kilroy.

XI

THE HURRICANE STRIKES

SHORTLY AFTER TEN THIRTY THAT morning, there came a sudden lull in the driving northeast wind and rain. Looking up from the table where she was preparing clams and vegetables for a chowder, Mrs. Greene observed the lull and decided that it would be a good chance to go outside and get some more wood from the shed for the range. Without even bothering to don a shawl or raincoat, she opened the kitchen door, which faced toward the west, and left it open so that she could enter there more easily with her armful of wood. Beyond the steps, after a few feet, the ground was two or three inches deep with unabsorbed rainwater, which was unusual in that sandy soil. She wished she had stopped to put on her rubbers but did not go back to get them.

Weather-wise, after many years of watching the changes in atmosphere, she noticed the heavy, warm quality of the air and especially its strange stillness after the roaring blow of the last twelve hours. Sniffing it suspiciously, she muttered, "I don't like it somehow. Wind's dropped and it's going to change—but not for the better, I figure. Funny smell to the air. I wish they was all back in the house!"

Splashing back toward the house, she had almost reached the kitchen steps with her armful of wood when, with a screeching sound, the wind suddenly whipped around to the northwest, striking at her back with a fury she had never dreamed possible. Stumbling almost to her knees, she dropped the wood, and without stopping to pick it up, she scrambled up the kitchen steps, tore open the door, which had slammed shut, and was inside—and not a moment too soon, for a huge old willow tree that had stood for fifty years shading the west side of the house had suddenly snapped in two, and the upper part had fallen directly across the path she had, the very instant before, been taking toward the house.

Mrs. Greene leaned against the kitchen door, dizzy and panting for breath. Used as she had been through the years to shock and emergency of many kinds, she had never encountered anything quite like this. Escape from certain death had been for her only a matter of seconds, and the realization left her with a furious thumping heart and pulse. Steps pounding down the stairs warned of the coming of Monsieur, and she suddenly straightened up, proudly desirous of not showing anything but her usual calm and poise. The professor barged in, disheveled from disturbed sleep and utterly at a loss to fathom what the racket and excitement was all about. At the same moment, Thusy, who had been very listless all morning, roused also and screeched:

"Don't get excited!—Don't get excited!—Don't get—"

"Oh that bird!" cried Mrs. Greene, hastily disengaging him from his perch and thrusting him into his cage, at the same time covering it with a dark shawl. From that time on, he was silent.

"Vat ees all zis?" demanded Monsieur. "Me, I hear one awful cr-rash!"

"It's just the storm taking a turn for the worse," Mrs. Greene informed him. "Wind suddenly dropped and then whipped around northwest. Knocked over that old willow out there. I'm right sorry to see it go, too. My husband planted that fifty years ago. It was big and old, and I know they get awful rotten inside." She said not a word about her own narrow escape. Monsieur peered out of the window at the tree lying sprawled like a fallen giant directly across the path to the kitchen door. At the same instant, the rain began again in a torrential driving force that neither of them had ever seen equaled. It seemed to descend, not in separate drops, but in a solid sheet, driving by the relentless force of the gale. They stood gazing at it in wordless amazement.

Suddenly Monsieur demanded, "Vere ees Ted?"

The question roused Mrs. Greene to a fuller realization of conditions, and she quavered, "I—I don't know! He and Marty went out quite a while ago to look around the barn and—and see if they could find any trace of Chips. They haven't come back—so they must be there yet—unless—they went somewhere else! Oh! I do hope they aren't out in *this*!"

The information roused Monsieur to instant action. "Ah!" he cried. "Zey must not be left to get back alone! Me—I get some storm clothes on and go to help zem! Zis wind—eet ees terrible—zee barn—eet might blow down—"

At this moment there was a loud knocking at the front door of the house, on the opposite side to the kitchen. This door had not been unlocked since the night before. Mrs. Greene hurried through the hall to open it, saying as she went, "Mebbe that's them now."

It was not them, however, but her son, Captain Cy, who slid in the instant the door was opened and slammed it after him. He was breathless from struggling through the storm, and his slicker, sou'wester, and boots shed rivers of water as he strode through the hall to the kitchen.

"I come to tell you all," he said, "to keep indoors—every one of you! Weather Bureau has just sent out full gale warning—the worst storm we've ever had, I figure! It's that hurricane, come up from Florida. Yesterday they said it was going out to sea, but it turned somewhere on the way and began heading for the coast. I come over to see if you were all right—had a terrible time getting here at that! I see your old willow blew down; glad it didn't hit the house.

Blocks up your back doorway a bit—so I come in this way. What's the matter, anyhow?" he ended, for they were both staring at him with stark consternation in their faces.

"Matter enough!" said Mrs. Greene grimly. "Ted and Marty are both out somewhere—and Mr. Burnett went up to town earlier this morning. Hasn't got back yet either."

Captain Cy was instantly and deeply concerned. "Mr. Burnett can take care of himself, I figure, but where did those two youngsters go? We've got to see about them!"

"They went out to the barn—a long while ago—to look for—something," hesitated Mrs. Greene, "and they haven't come back. That was before the wind changed. I don't know whether they're there still or not."

"Well, I'll go straight out there and steer 'em in!" decided Captain Cy. "No use going out the kitchen way—path's all blocked up by that tree. I'll use the front door and go around." He strapped his sou'wester tighter against the wind, and his mother let him out the front door. Then she and Monsieur watched anxiously from a window as he plowed his way around the house, head bent to the tearing wind and rain. It seemed to the anxious watchers as if it took him at least ten minutes to cover the comparatively short space to the barn, into whose entrance he presently vanished. The moments until he reappeared seemed endless. And when he did, at last, come into view again, he was alone!

"Mebbe he thought it best to leave 'em there till the worst of this is over," Mrs. Greene said comfortingly to Monsieur, who literally began tearing at his hair at the sight. "That old barn's pretty solid. I guess they'd be safe enough there, for a while." Both of them were slightly encouraged by this thought as they watched Captain Cy battle his way back to the house.

"Are they all right?" cried Mrs. Greene as she once more admitted his dripping figure.

"They ain't there!" he groaned. "I looked in every corner and hollered and shouted. Nary a sign of them!" The blow of this information seemed more than could be borne. At the same moment, there came from outdoors a sudden crack like a cannon shot, and through the window they beheld the upper half of a great, stately red cedar, a short distance from the house, broken off jaggedly and hurtled to the ground.

Falteringly, Mrs. Greene suggested, "Mebbe they went over to the station—and are in there. It would be a likely place they might go."

"It's a chance," acknowledged the captain, "though I think I'd have seen 'em if they had. Anyhow, I'll go back there and look. And if they ain't, I'm going to call up the coast guards from South Inlet and tell 'em they'll have to come up here and help hunt. And don't you two stir out of this house! You can't do any good, and it'd only make more people getting in danger and having to be hunted up. If Mr. Burnett comes in, tell him he'd better stay indoors, too. Same thing applies to *him*! This kind of thing is what the coast guards are for—and they know how to do it better'n anybody else." He jerked open the door after this advice and was gone, leaving two elderly and very frightened people staring at each other.

Though they both knew that the Captain's advice was wise, they found it exceedingly hard to follow. Monsieur raged up and down the kitchen, tearing at his hair and muttering that he *must* go out and help to rescue "zose poor children" left at the mercy of the storm.

Mrs. Greene was at her wits' end to restrain him, and that prompted her to reply rather tartly, "Do stop worrying so much about them! After all, Marty's good and strong, and she knows her way about this place almost better'n I do, who have lived here all my life. She'll find places they can crawl into and be safe—she ain't going to let Ted come to any harm!" Suddenly her attention was distracted by drops of water oozing down from a crack in the kitchen ceiling.

"Look at *that*! It's leaking in somewhere upstairs," she moaned. "Better come up and help me, Professor. It'll be something we can do while we're waiting."

Eager to be of some help, Monsieur agreed, and they were

soon toiling upstairs armed with pails and mopping cloths. The condition they found there more than verified Mrs. Greene's worst predictions. At every window on the north and west sides, water was seeping in rapidly, not only under the sills but under the very window frames also. Pools of it had gathered on the floors beneath them and were slowly but surely spreading wider and wider over the floors. In addition to that, a none-too-waterproof roof had betrayed them, and a steady stream was coming down through the ceilings in almost every room.

Frantically they worked moving beds and other furniture, rolling up rugs, placing pails and basins where they would catch the ceiling leaks, and mopping futilely at the ever-widening pools that were creeping across the floors from the windows. In the midst of their labors, there came another furious knocking at the front door, and their hopes were raised anew that Captain Cy had at last found the wandering youngsters. It was not Captain Cy, however, as they found when they had both descended to open the door. It was Mr. Burnett, drenched and spent after battling his way back from town.

"I never was so glad to get indoors in my life!" he panted, half-laughingly, as the door was closed and he stood dripping in the hall. "I thought I'd never get here alive! This is the *real thing*—and no joke at that! I was fortunate enough to get a ride down on the South Inlet Coast Guard truck. They tell me it's the Florida hurricane. What a pity your big old tree has come down, Mrs. Greene!"

The two stood facing him—silent. Neither could find words in which to break to him what they knew he must soon be told. It was Mrs. Greene who presently asked him in a dull voice if he had seen Captain Cy on his way over from the beach. Frantically she hoped that perhaps he *had* and therefore might have learned that the children were safe. But he only replied:

"No, I didn't come by his house. You see, I didn't fancy coming through the lane, where a branch from one of those trees might crack down on me any minute, so I got them to let me off a little farther north, where I came in a sort of roundabout way over those back dunes. It was almost impossible going, bucking that terrific wind and rain, but I made it—somehow! By the way, where's Ted? I have a letter for him."

It had to come at last. There was no evading the issue now. Mr. Burnett sensed that something was wrong by the expressions on their stricken faces. In a flat monotone, which she had to employ to keep from bursting into tears, Mrs. Greene outlined the history, so far as she knew it, of Ted and Marty's morning.

Mr. Burnett's face turned a little gray as she ended, but his voice bore not a trace of excitement as he gravely replied, "Don't be alarmed. This sounds fairly serious, but it may not be as bad as you think. I'll wait here ten minutes longer for Captain Cy to return. I'm sure he'll do so, in any case. Then, if he hasn't found the children over at the station, I'm going back with him to help hunt them up. You, Monsieur, must stay here with Mrs. Greene. She cannot be left alone in this crisis. And don't worry! They can't possibly have gotten so far away that we can't find them if we go at it systematically. They may even walk in here while we're still looking for them—you never can tell!"

His cheerful words heartened them a bit, and at that moment Captain Cy again entered by at the front door. Hopefully, they all turned to him, but he shook his head.

"Sorry, but they haven't been near the station, seems like, and no one's seen 'em around. I've called the lower coast guards, and they'll be up as soon as the truck gets back. Mr. Burnett, you better stay here."

But Mr. Burnett shook his head and announced, "I'll go with you, Captain Cy. You wouldn't expect me to sit in the house when my boy and Marty are out in—*this*!"

The Captain understood and said no more except to suggest that they take along a couple of blankets and some lengths of rope. And when these were procured, they both went out into the storm, leaving Mrs. Greene and Monsieur staring forlornly after them.

XII

ON THE TRAIL OF CHIPS

"Marty, what does Chips really look like?" demanded Ted as they splashed along the path through the woods toward the bay. "I didn't get a really good look at him last Sunday when he came over to the beach with his mother. We were too busy hiding from them!" he ended with a chuckle.

"Well, he's a sort of overgrown boy for his age," described Marty. "He's only fifteen—same age as I am—but he looks as if he were eighteen or nineteen nearly. He has black hair and very black, thick eyebrows. He isn't at all good looking, only he has nice eyes—gray ones, and when he's in a good humor, he has a nice expression. But mostly he's scowling and cross looking. He's very strong. And he's very clever with his fingers, too—carves beautiful little figures out of wood. And he's smart, too. He's got a good brain, only he never gets any time to study at home, and that keeps him way behind in his grades. He goes to the same high school I do, and I've helped him sometimes with his work because I felt rather sorry for him. Most of the others are mean to him—tease him so much."

Ted considered this description carefully. "Somehow, he doesn't seem like the sort of boy who would try to do a mean thing like stealing Thusy, does he?"

"He mightn't think of it as *stealing*—not if his mother had made him believe Thusy really belonged to them," suggested Marty. And Ted had to admit that might be so.

All the while they had been splashing along, somewhat sheltered from the driving northeast wind and rain by the trees and shrubbery. They had been glancing about, right and left of the path, to discover with certainty whether this was surely the way Chips had come. But the soaking rain, which the sand seemed unable to absorb, lay about in puddles and practically obliterated any footprints. Only once, as they were nearing the edge of the bay, did they discover a heel print that might or might not have been that of their quarry.

The water of the bay, close by the sandy beach, was singularly calm. Only out beyond, where the wind had a clear sweep, could they see gust after gust tearing across the troubled water and white-crested rollers surging toward the southwest.

"What do you suppose Chips came over here for?" questioned Ted, scanning the shore both north and south for any sign of the boy.

"I think I can guess," ventured Marty sagely. "He knows he can't hide in the barn during the daytime. We'd certainly find him. So he must have planned to come over to the bay shore. I think I know just the place where he could stay and nobody'd find him—unless they happened to be hunting for him, as we are."

"Where's *that*?" demanded Ted in great excitement. "We might creep up on him and catch him!"

"I wonder just what we'd do if we *did* catch him?" chuckled Marty suddenly, as the thought occurred to her. "I'm sure *I* don't know! He's big enough to throw both of us into the bay if he felt like it!"

This was rather a poser, but Ted stoutly maintained, "We could ask him what he's over here for in all this storm, anyway, and—and if there's any way we could help him. He'd have to think of *something* to answer to that."

Marty agreed that it might have some result, and, in any case, since he would then be aware that they knew he was prowling about, he mightn't think it worthwhile to stay any longer.

"But you haven't told me yet where you thought he might be hiding over here in the daytime," Ted reminded her.

"Oh, no, I haven't," she agreed. "Well, my guess is that he's gone farther along down the shore. Uncle Cy does a lot of fishing in the bay in his spare time. He has a couple of rowboats and some nets and crab cars, and he built a little shed to keep oars and nets and tools in, down farther. It's a little place, not even high enough to stand up straight in, but anyone could crawl in there and be out of sight and under cover from the storm. It hasn't any lock, so Chips could get in there easily if he wanted to. It's a ways farther down—in the cove where we landed the boat yesterday. You can't see it from here. The next point of land is in the way."

"Well, let's go down there then," demanded Ted. "We can creep up on him quietly, and he'll never know we're around till we face him!"

Even while thinking about other things, Marty could not help but note the change in the shy and timid boy of a few days ago. She couldn't then have imagined him making any such bold suggestion. And since the rain and wind seemed to be slacking a bit, she agreed that it might be all right to go along the shore and investigate her uncle's little shelter. It rather intrigued her to imagine what the hiding Chips might do if they were to suddenly confront him in his temporary lair—if it chanced that he was really there at all.

After they had rounded the point, Marty suggested that they had better proceed as much as possible behind the bushes and trees that lined the shore, as it would keep them out of sight of the little shelter. For if Chips should see them approaching, he might leave it and run off into the woods. It was not easy going, for vines and tangled undergrowth impeded their progress. But they managed to cover a certain distance until they came to a very marshy spot.

"We'll have to go out and around this," warned Marty. "It's

one of those places where you sink over your knees the minute you step into it. There are quite a number of these spots along the shore. Some are so bad that you sink into them completely if you're not careful—almost like quicksand. It'll be harder ground out by the water, but I hope he doesn't see us when we come out of the bushes."

They emerged cautiously into the open and glanced toward the shelter, which was now not much farther from them than a hundred yards. But as they looked, Marty's surmise was verified. A dark, hulking figure that had been lurking on the far side of it bolted suddenly into the woods and was lost to sight.

"There he is!" breathed Ted. "You were right. He must have seen us first when we came around the point and has been watching ever since to see if we'd come nearer. Hurry! Let's try to chase him." And Ted was off down the beach before Marty could remonstrate.

Hurriedly she scrambled after him, surprised at his fleetness, even hampered as he was by heavy boots and clinging slicker. Watching him dart into the bushes, she had not paid heed to her own steps, and suddenly her foot tripped on a projecting branch that was partly embedded in the sand, and she fell headlong, wrenching her ankle quite painfully in the fall.

For several moments she lay there, jarred clear through and in too much real pain to get up.

"Oh, *why* did this have to happen?" she thought, irritated at her own clumsiness or lack of watchfulness. "I do hope I haven't sprained my ankle! And Ted's tearing away—farther every minute! He mustn't! He might get lost!"

Painfully she raised herself on one elbow and shouted, "Ted! Ted!" She listened, straining to hear an answer, but there came none. By this time he must be too far away to hear, or else the noise of the storm had carried her voice in another direction.

"Oh well," she thought, "he can't very well lose himself. Only I wish he hadn't rushed off that way. I'm certain he won't catch up with Chips, and he'll come on back when he gets tired of it. My ankle hurts like everything! I think I'll take this heavy boot off and see what's wrong with it."

She sat up with some difficulty. The force of her sudden fall seemed to have jarred and bruised every muscle in her body. With considerable difficulty, she managed to remove the rubber boot and rubbed the aching ankle for several minutes. It seemed to be swelling some, but as she could wiggle her foot quite freely, she decided that no bones were broken and that it was only a painful wrench.

"It'll be a job—limping home on this," she considered. "I do wish Ted would come back! Wherever can he have got to?" She called again, several times, but received no answer, so she decided she had better replace the boot, try to find Ted, and get home as speedily as possible.

Getting the boot back on was a painful process since the ankle seemed to be swelling fast. However, it was accomplished at last, and by getting to her knees first and then standing on the uninjured foot, she tried her weight on it, gingerly. With a little "ouch!" of pain, she found she could bear her weight on it and limp along, though she could see that the trip home was going to be no picnic. Now, if Ted would only come, they could set about getting back.

As she stood there waiting for him, she was suddenly aware that it had stopped raining and blowing and that a curious dead calm had set in. The air had an odd odor, and she sniffed it curiously.

"The wind's going to change," she thought. "I hope this storm's over, but I don't think I ever knew the air to smell so strange! Anyhow, I'm thankful it isn't raining and blowing anymore. It'll be hard enough getting back on this lame foot of mine without having to buck the storm, too!"

Minutes passed, and Ted had not yet returned. Marty began to worry about him now and wonder what she ought to do.

"It doesn't seem as if I *could* go hunting him up through the underbrush—with this ankle—and yet, it doesn't seem right to just let him disappear like that without doing anything about it. Besides,

I might miss him, and we'd just be wandering around hunting each other up. Maybe it's more sensible to stay right here till he gets back. He *can't* have found Chips—that boy would be at the other end of the island before he'd let anyone catch up with him!"

At that moment, an awful thought occurred to her. "Oh! The *bog*!" she cried aloud in alarm. "That dreadful old bog farther down—the worst one on this side of the bay! If he should be running—and step into that without noticing it—" She couldn't finish the dreadful thought, even to herself. But it settled the matter of hunting up Ted—at once—even if her ankle was very painful. Deciding that it would be best to make her way along the shore and shout to him at intervals, instead of plunging into the thick undergrowth and floundering about in it, she turned to hobble south along the narrow strip of land.

It was at this instant that a howling, shrieking wind, coming from the northwest across the bay, struck her squarely in the back and sent her reeling to her knees. The force and suddenness of it were like nothing she had ever experienced before, but thinking it only a sudden gust of the changing wind, she lay flat on the sand for a moment, waiting for it to blow over.

But it didn't blow over! Instead of subsiding as she had expected, it grew steadily worse, pressing her down on the sand with its impact. Added to that, great rollers from the bay began slashing at the shore, showering her with spray and presently coming nearer to roll over her feet. And, as a last straw, the very heavens seemed to open, and torrents of rain, driven almost horizontally by the terrific wind, poured down on her in stinging sheets. Marty had experienced a goodly number of severe storms in her life, but never anything like this!

Dazed with its terrific force, she lay where she was, unable to concentrate on what to do, until a great wave rolled halfway over her, and she knew she must at once get away from this close proximity to the shore. Drenched and so beaten by the unhampered strength of the wind from across the bay that she actually could not have stood upright, she managed to crawl painfully through the seagrass and in behind the scant protection of the heavy underbrush and cedars that lined the shore. Still hoping it might only be a severe but temporary squall, she rested there for a few moments in the shelter of a twisted old cedar tree and wondered frantically what was happening to Ted.

"As soon as this is over," she told herself, "I'll go and hunt him up if it kills me! Could this be the hurricane that Mr. Burnett was joking about only yesterday? O, God, keep Ted safe till I can get to him!" she prayed inwardly.

Hopeful, she waited for the longed-for slackening in the sudden tempest. Surely it must come soon! Such a fury of rain and wind couldn't last very long! But far from slackening, it seemed to grow steadily worse. Never in her life had she heard such a frightful screaming of wind or felt such torrents of rain, driven in literal horizontal sheets. She could not even open her mouth to breathe unless her head was turned in the opposite direction from it. In fact, she dared not move from the slight protection of the sheltering old tree, lest she be rolled helplessly before the driving tornado.

Spent, shivering, drenched to the bone, and filled with nameless terrors for the wandering Ted, she clung to the protecting trunk, too dazed and miserable even for any constructive thought, praying only that this tempest might cease—and soon!

Suddenly, with no warning save a curious, muffled, rending sound, the great, twisted, leaning old cedar that had weathered two centuries of storm keeled over—its roots literally torn out of the ground—and swayed to earth. Marty, who had been crouching against the lower part of its trunk, felt it quiver and heard the rending sound and knew instinctively what was coming. With a little cry, she got on her knees and tried to scramble away from the direction in which she knew it would fall. Had her ankle not been injured, she would have been on her feet and out of danger before it came down, in all likelihood. But, hampered as she was, to crawl away was the only alternative.

But she was not quick enough. Though the main body of the tree escaped her, a great, curving branch caught her before she was quite out of its range and pinned her to the ground. Singularly enough, it did her no great physical injury, for the main weight of it was supported by the masses of thickly leaved smaller branches and miraculously did not touch her. But she was caught, nevertheless, inextricably, among these smaller branches and could not pull herself out in any direction. After struggling in vain for several minutes, she knew with certainty that she could never be freed without outside help. But where was that help coming from? Who would know where she and Ted had strayed that morning? And where was Ted himself? Caught, perhaps, in some even worse predicament than her own?

The cruelly slashing rain and the screaming wind were growing even worse. She could not call for help against them. There was no one within half a mile who could give any help, anyway. She could have stood it all, she felt, if only she could know that Ted was safe.

After a while she slipped into merciful unconsciousness, the roaring hurricane still hurtling over her as she lay pinned under the cedar tree.

XIII

HURRICANE'S HARVEST

At two o'clock that afternoon, Mrs. Greene sat down in her comfortable old rocker in the kitchen and despairingly wiped her face, which was streaming with perspiration. The kitchen was the only comparatively dry room in the house. The window whose broken pane had been removed by Chips that morning she had closed by shutting tight the outside shutter and filling up the chinks with cloths.

She was weary and disheartened and, not for the first time in her life, frightened almost out of her wits. This latter state of mind, however, she would rather have died than reveal. Monsieur sat in another chair by the table, resting his forehead in his hands and breathing an occasional deep sigh. Both were long past any words to describe their emotions. Not since Mr. Burnett and Captain Cy had left them around noon had they had a moment's respite or a moment of encouragement. Every hour the hurricane had grown worse. The house shook on its very foundations, the windows fairly bulged inward from the force of the blast, and the house was drenched from top to bottom with the rain that had been driven into every nook and cranny, under every doorsill, beneath every window, and through many suspected and unsuspected leaky spots in the roof.

These two elderly people, working like beavers, had rolled up all the rugs, covered mattresses on beds, stored furniture in obscure corners to be free from dripping ceilings, and mopped floors till at last they had had to give that up. The more they mopped, the more rain had streamed in, till now it was even running down the stairs from the upper story. The screaming of the wind and the crash of driven rain created a racket that was deafening. And every once in a while, a sound like a cannon shot told that another tree or great branch of one had gone to the ground.

And all the while, there had been never a word of Ted and Marty, nor even of those who had gone to find them in this fury of hurricane. Both of them feared the worst yet would not voice their fears. Mrs. Greene glanced up at an old barometer that had belonged to her husband and which hung on the wall over the kitchen table. It registered 27°, and she shuddered and looked away. Never, in the worst storm she had ever remembered, had it registered less than 29° or a fraction below. She did not call Monsieur's attention to it. It wouldn't help matters any, she considered.

At last, when she was a trifle rested, she rose and went to the range, coming back with a pot of steaming coffee that she had prepared some time before.

"We better drink some coffee and eat a bite," she said in a lifeless voice. "Do us both good—even if we don't feel like it. I've got some hot soup, too, in that kettle. We'll eat that and some bread and butter, and I'll keep the soup and coffee hot for the others when they come in."

"Ah! I cannot eat wis zis so dreadful sing going on!" moaned Monsieur. But she placed the food before him, nevertheless, and insisted that he try. Presently they had both made some sort of a meal and felt greatly refreshed with the hot soup and steaming coffee. Things even began to seem a bit more hopeful. And

Monsieur suggested that any time now, the wanderers must surely be coming in, and that since they could do no more toward keeping the house dry, they might watch out the windows to see from which direction they might emerge.

"Well, you do the watching," Mrs. Greene had advised. "I better go and get a couple of beds fixed with dry sheets and blankets. If those children have been out so long in this, they'll be chilled to the bone, as well as being soaked, and ought to be put straight to bed." And so saying, she went off on her errand while Monsieur roamed disconsolately from window to window, through most of which he could see nothing, for the solid sheets of rain blurred all vision beyond the panes.

Half an hour later, however, there came a terrific thumping on the front door. And, calling excitedly up the stairs to Mrs. Greene, Monsieur rushed to open it. The sight that met his eyes caused him to cry out in dismay. Two drenched young coast guards stood there, bearing between them a blanket. And in that blanket rested the dripping and apparently lifeless form of Marty.

"Don't worry!" they advised him as they carried her in. "She isn't dead—only hurt a bit. Where'd we better put her?"

"Bring her right upstairs!" called out Mrs. Greene, who was already halfway down. "I got a warm bed ready for her." They wasted no words but bore her up in the blanket.

"But—but where ees Ted—zee boy?" gasped Monsieur as they clattered down again and were about to rush out once more.

The young men wiped their streaming faces and explained, "We haven't found him yet. We came across the girl first and brought her right back. But don't worry, probably they'll have found him by the time we get back. He'll be all right—no fear! But this sure is *some* storm!"

They felt there was no time for more words and were gone before Monsieur could put another question. Hurrying upstairs, he found that Mrs. Greene had put Marty in her own bed—the room being drier and more comfortable than the one Marty had been using.

"Tell me, what can I do?" he whispered when she had opened the door at his tap. "Ees—ees she badly hurt?"

"I don't think so," answered Mrs. Greene, her eyes alight with some measure of happiness now that she had at least her beloved granddaughter back safely. "She's almost too tuckered out to speak, and she has a sprained ankle—couldn't walk—and a lot of bruises—but I guess she'll be all right. You can bring up a kettle of hot water, if you'll be so kind."

"But—but did she say anysing about—*Ted*?" Monsieur faltered. He felt that he *must* know that before he took another step.

"All she said was to ask if he'd got back yet," admitted Mrs. Greene. "She said she lost him—he ran off just before the hurricane broke. That's all I know so far. Mebbe when she feels a little better, she'll tell us more about it."

He had to be content with that, and the next half hour he spent climbing up and down stairs and running various errands of help, carrying hot water, hot coffee, hot soup, and other necessaries, while Mrs. Greene hovered over Marty with every restorative at her command. Finally she announced that Marty seemed to be recovering her strength and was more like herself. She wanted the girl to go to sleep, but Marty insisted that she wanted to tell them all about her adventure, and so Monsieur and Mrs. Greene sat by her bed and listened while, in a weak voice, Marty told what had transpired since she and Ted had left in the morning to hunt for traces of Chips in the barn.

"It—it was terrible—after the tree fell on me!" she half sobbed. "It wasn't that it hurt me so much—it didn't—only bruised me some. But I was just pinned there—I couldn't get away—I couldn't try to find Ted. I was worried sick about him. And the terrible rain and wind—and those tangled tree branches holding me down so I couldn't move—it was like a nightmare, worse than any I ever had. I didn't think anyone would ever find me till after I was drowned with the rain. I kept losing myself every little while—like a faint—and when I'd come to, it was just as bad as ever—or worse! The rain kept making the puddle of water I was lying in deeper and deeper. I had to hold my head high to keep my face out of it. That's why I thought I might drown. Then suddenly, I thought I heard just a little sound over the noise of the wind, like voices shouting. It seemed as if they must be quite near, or I couldn't have heard them. I just sort of got together all the strength I had left—and screamed and yelled 'Help!' till I was hoarse.

"And Mr. Burnett heard me! He was with the coast guards and came running over to the tree. I'd nearly fainted again by that time, but I yelled just once more—and he knew I was buried under that big branch, almost down under the water. Then they all got together and lifted the branch and dragged me out. I wanted to wait till they found Ted, but Mr. Burnett made two of the coast guards carry me home. But, oh! *What* can have become of Ted?" she ended with a moan, burying her head in the pillow.

"There, there!" Mrs. Greene soothed her. "Don't you keep fretting about that! They'll find him, same as they found you—and bring him home all right. You drink the rest of this hot soup, and then you go to sleep. You're just nigh exhausted, that's all." She forced Marty to drink the soup and sent Monsieur downstairs to watch for the return of the others. Then she sat by the bedside till Marty had dropped off into the sleep of sheer exhaustion, then crept down to join Monsieur in his vigil.

Another hour crept by—and nothing further had happened. The barometer still stood at 27°. The hurricane had not abated one whit. In fact, it seemed worse than ever! There had been no sign or word of Ted and those who sought him. As the two sat disconsolately in the kitchen, saying little, starting at every fresh blast of wind and rain, Mrs. Greene suddenly moved to glance once more at the old barometer. And, having done so, she gave a little gasp of surprise. For the indicator had moved upward from 27° until it stood almost at 28°!

"Oh, thank the Lord!" she murmured, almost unconsciously. "It's *going up!*"

"Vat ees eet?" demanded Monsieur in a startled tone. And Mrs. Greene joyfully pointed out the barometer to him and explained its workings while he listened and watched the indicator in fascinated wonder.

"I don't think I ever saw it at 27° in my life before," she explained. "Abner always used to tell me that if it ever got there, we could expect the worst—but that it probably never would, in these parts. They get that down south in the hurricane regions. But it was there today, all right! Only I didn't want to scare you by saying anything about it. But it's going up—do you see! And I do believe the storm is slackening a bit!" They both hurried to a window and tried to peer through the rain-dimmed panes. Certainly it seemed to be coming down less viciously, and the wind had lost some of its furious screaming.

For a time the miracle took their thoughts away from the immediate problem of the unreturned wanderers, and they watched the slowly rising needle with fascinated gaze. In another twenty minutes, the needle had risen to 29°, the wind had dropped to what would be only the force of an ordinary northeaster, and the rain had diminished to little more than usual storm proportions. And while they were watching this amazing change, they were suddenly startled by the sound of clumping feet on the front veranda. Both of them immediately hurried to the front door and opened it.

Four dripping, disheveled people stood there. Two of them were Mr. Burnett and Captain Cy, both exhausted looking but grinning broadly. The third was Ted, minus his sou'wester and—strangely enough—his *boots*, his big blue eyes sparkling with a mischievous twinkle. And lastly, a black-haired, black-browed, hulking figure who was sheepishly loath to enter with the others.

It was none other than the elusive and dour Chips!

XIV

AFTER THE STORM

"WELL! I JUST DON'T UNDERSTAND it all!" muttered Mrs. Greene, taking off her spectacles and wiping them for the third time as she rocked nervously in her old kitchen rocker. The last surprise of this terrifying day had been almost too much for her. From the moment that she had beheld Ted alive, alive and unharmed, the strength borne of excitement and suspense had seemed to ooze out of her, leaving her trembling and shaken. The arrival of Chips with the party had been the most astonishing of all the strange events.

Captain Cy had waited only long enough to ascertain that Marty was unharmed and recovering and that the older people were in no trouble except that caused by the leakage and disruption of the house, and had then hurriedly departed, explaining that he was worried about his own wife and young daughter who had been alone in their home all during the hurricane and must be needing him. He had left all explanations to the rest of the rescue party. Mr. Burnett had hurried Ted and Chips upstairs to get them into dry clothes (volunteering to lend Chips some of his own), and Monsieur had gone with them to assist. Mr. Burnett had postponed all accounts of their adventures till they came down again. It was then that Mrs. Greene had retired to her rocker to collect her wits and rest her trembling limbs. Marty, deep in the sleep of sheer exhaustion, had not even roused at their entrance.

Now they had come trooping back into the kitchen, and explanations were in order, as was also the refreshment of food and hot coffee. A silent and plainly rather terrified Chips, looking somewhat odd in a sweater and trousers of Mr. Burnett's, hung back in the rear and acted very ill at ease.

"I see you have a pot of coffee on the range," laughed Mr. Burnett to Mrs. Greene, "and if we might have some now, I'll tell you all about it. And please let me explain right here that Chips is a most welcome guest and has earned my eternal gratitude. It was he who rescued Ted from a terrible predicament. I salute you, Chips, as a real hero!"

The boy blushed furiously, shuffled his feet, and muttered, "It wasn't anything but what anyone would do!" But Mr. Burnett disagreed with that and insisted that he sit down with them at the table, while Mrs. Greene got up and hurried about to provide them with food and coffee. Ted, meanwhile, was obviously bubbling over with the desire to tell his side of the affair and burst out:

"Chips certainly *did* save my life, and I want to tell about it. Dad hasn't heard it all, anyway, though he knows some about it. I guess Marty must have told you how we followed Chips to the bay and saw him run into the woods. I ran ahead, thinking she was close behind me, but I didn't see her again—and I don't know just what happened to her before the tree fell on her. Dad told me about that. I was sure she'd catch up with me somehow, so I just ran on. Chips was ducking behind trees and dunes. I'd catch a glimpse of him every once in a while, but I never could catch up with him. My big rubber boots kept me from running as fast as I could have. Chips didn't have boots, so he could keep well ahead of me. And then, all of a sudden, something awful happened!" Ted looked very solemn and took a sip of hot coffee. Then he continued:

"I wasn't looking where I was going—I was watching to get another glimpse of Chips—when I suddenly stepped into something terribly soft, like water and mud. But I was going so fast I couldn't stop myself till I'd gone two or three steps farther in it and about three or four feet from solid ground. The more I tried to get out, the deeper I sank, till I was up over my knees. Then I knew I must be in one of those bogs Marty had told me about. I was *so* near the solid ground—and yet I couldn't reach it! The more I tried, the deeper I went till I was up to my waist. Then I called for help and screamed and screamed. I thought Marty must be somewhere near—but no one answered. I guess the wind carried my voice away. Even calling out seemed to make me go deeper, so I kept perfectly still. I thought Marty might find me before I sank too deep. I was awfully scared!" He shuddered, and the others shuddered with him, realizing his horrible plight. But Ted shook himself as if to throw off the dreadful memory, smiled, and went on:

"I don't know how long I stayed there—all alone and sinking in farther all the time. It seemed like hours, but I guess it wasn't. All of a sudden, I saw someone coming over a dune just a little way off. I knew it was Chips—and I was so afraid he might run off again because I'd been chasing him. So I kept perfectly quiet till he could get nearer and see the fix I was in. I was sure he wouldn't leave me just to—just to—disappear—in the mud. But I needn't have worried about it, for he saw me—all by himself—and came running around near to where I was.

"I called to him to help me if he could, and all he said was, 'Hold on, buddy, and don't move! I'm going to give you a hand, soon as I find something you can grab onto.' Then he went running around looking for something, and at last he came back dragging a long, slender tree that had fallen over, with some of its roots still on the bottom. He said it was pretty tough because it wasn't a dead tree—hadn't been down very long. Then he asked me if I had on rubber boots or just shoes. I told him boots, and he said to reach down, if I could, and try to unfasten the straps of them. I couldn't seem to get at them without sinking deeper. They were below the water and mud. So he slid out the tree, with the root end toward me, and told me to hang on to that with one hand and unfasten the straps with the other, if I could.

"I grabbed some of the roots while he hung on to the other end, and it held me up much better. But I thought I'd never get those straps unfastened. I didn't see why he wanted me to bother with them—not till later. At last I did, though, and then he told me to hang on to those roots with both hands, for dear life, and not to let go even if it pulled my arms off! So I hung on, and he took the other end of the tree and began to pull. It didn't budge me a bit, and I thought my arms would tear right off me. Then Chips said:

"'It's those boots! Kick at 'em! Try to get free of 'em!' And then I knew why he'd wanted me to unbuckle the tops. So, while he pulled again, I kicked and wriggled my feet till I'd got 'em free of that part around the ankle. And then all of a sudden, Chips gave one great big tug—and I came out of 'em—and he hauled me up on the bank that was firm! It's good you got me those boots a size and a half larger than I needed, Dad, so I could grow into them, or—or they never would have come off!" He drew a long sigh at this point, and the others also breathed more freely after the tension of listening to that thrilling rescue. Only Chips wriggled in his chair, did not seem to know where to look, and acted most uncomfortable generally.

"But zen, vat do you do?" demanded Monsieur, leaning forward to lay a tender clasp on one of Ted's bruised and scratched hands. In his heart he wondered how much damage had been done to those precious hands and whether or not it would interfere with the boy's piano work. But he said no word of that, only adding, "Vere you stay zen—in all zis so dreadful storm? Vy do you not come straight home?"

"That's another part of the story," laughed Ted. "We hadn't been noticing the weather at all while Chips was trying to get me out. I think it had stopped raining and blowing, but we had too much else to think about. All of a sudden, while I was lying on the solid ground, trying to get my breath and waiting for the dreadful aching in my arms to stop, the wind came screaming at us like mad, and it began to rain so hard—I'd never seen anything like it! We were in a sort of hollow and got a little protection from the wind, but the rain just came at us in sheets, and the water in that marshy place began to rise. We knew we couldn't stay there, and I said I better be trying to get home and asked Chips if he would help me. He said:

"'You aren't ever going to get to Greenes' facing this wind. I've never seen anything like it. Comes right *at* you, going in that direction! Besides, you haven't any boots now—can't travel far through the brambles in your stocking feet. You're a city chap, and your feet aren't used to it. I know a little old fisherman's shack a bit farther south—not very far. If we can get to that, we can have shelter till this thing blows over. We'll be traveling with the wind, not bucking it. You grab me around the neck, and I'll carry you pickaback. You aren't very heavy. We'll make it!'

"So I did as he said, and he took me on his back. It was a terrible trip, though! I don't know how we ever made it. The wind and the rain almost knocked Chips over plenty of times. And several times we had to lie flat on the ground while he rested and got his breath. But finally we got there. It was a funny, tiny little hut, hidden away in the bushes and sandhills, and I guess nobody'd lived in it for a long time. It was just one little room with two tiny windows and a door that wasn't locked. But we went in and shut the door and just lay on the floor for a while, trying to get rested up after that awful pull. Chips thought the storm would blow over after a while and he could take me home, but it didn't. It just kept getting worse and worse!

"After a while, when I could think about anything at all, I began to worry about Marty. I was afraid she'd be hunting for me, roaming around in all that awful blow. You see, I didn't know she'd hurt her ankle or what happened to her afterward. Chips thought she'd probably gone home and would get someone to help us. So we just lay there and rested, but nobody came. We didn't talk much. The noise of the storm was so loud you had to shout. Sometimes we thought the little house would blow over—it shook so much—but it didn't. And then, after hours and hours—so it seemed—Dad and Captain Cy and the coast guards found us!" Ted stopped for breath at this point, and Mr. Burnett took up the tale.

"Yes, we found them!" he went on. "And I don't need to tell you all that that was a happy moment. It was Captain Cy who suggested making our way down to that hut. He knew of it—had known of it for years—but the coast guards, who were young men rather new to this locality, didn't. The little hut is very well hidden and hasn't been occupied for a long time. So we battled our way to it through the storm—and had our reward! When we found the two boys safe and unharmed, Captain Cy and I decided to stay there with them till the worst of the storm was past, but the coast guards were anxious to be on their way, since there was no more they could do, and they left. We waited quite a long while, and the storm seemed to be getting worse instead of slackening. Suddenly one of the windows was blown in, and we all concluded that it wasn't safe to stay there any longer; the place might collapse over our heads. Captain Cy thought our best plan would be to make our way across to the ocean front, as the dunes would provide some protection from the wind, and that's what we did. Oddly enough, we found a pair of old, discarded rubber boots in a corner of the shack, and Ted put them on. They were miles too big for him and full of holes, but they did protect his feet, getting through the brambles, though they hampered his progress quite a bit.

"I don't like to think too much of that journey getting over to the beach. It was a nightmare, for the storm was at its worst. But we made it—somehow! When we got there, we crept along, close to the dunes, which gave us some protection. Ted discarded the old boots then, as the sand was easier to walk through without them. And before we reached there, there'd come a change, and Captain Cy said he thought the worst was over. By the time we reached the house, it had dwindled to just an ordinary rain and blow."

"And look at it *now!*" cried Ted, pointing to the west window. So absorbed had they all been in this saga of adventure during the hurricane that none had given a thought to the present state of the weather. A golden shaft of sun had dried the moisture on the panes, and a bright blue sky, almost cloudless, was visible up above. The trees had ceased to lash wildly, and the disordered earth was flooded with late afternoon sunlight.

For their portion of the world, at least, the hurricane of the century was a thing of the past!

XV

AFTERMATH

MARTY SAT ALONE IN THE kitchen by the table, peeling some potatoes for her grandmother. One foot was propped on a stool. The warm morning sunlight streamed through the windows, all open to an air as balmy as midsummer. She was alone as she worked. Mrs. Greene was upstairs trying to straighten affairs in her disordered house, Ted and Monsieur had gone over to the Coast Guard station to ascertain the condition of the pianos, Mr. Burnett had gone to town by way of walking up the beach, and Chips was out in the back chopping vigorously at the fallen willow tree, to remove its obstruction from the dooryard.

The memory of the nightmare that was yesterday still clung to Marty. She had not been able to shake it off entirely since she had awakened late the previous afternoon to learn that Ted was back, alive and safe, and to be told the history of his providential rescue by—of all people—the very Chips whom they had been chasing about as an objectionable intruder! Could it be possible they had actually thought he had been trying to make off with Thusy? The macaw was even now sitting on his perch near her, clucking and muttering contentedly to himself as he pecked at his seed dish—and Chips right outside the door, chopping like a Trojan at the branches of the fallen willow!

"What a topsy-turvy world!" she thought.

There had been few, if any, questions asked of Chips the previous evening. All of them, except herself, had been too busy trying to mop up the flooded house and restore some sort of order after the hurricane. And by common, though unspoken, consent, they had treated Chips as one of them, ignoring completely even the memory of the events of the night before.

There had been no question of his return to his own home. That was soon found to be impossible. Mr. Burnett had gone over to Captain Cy's house soon after the calm had arrived, only to find a most unlooked-for and appalling state of affairs on the oceanfront. A very high tide that had been due much earlier that day had been held out by the terrific force of the northwest wind. When the hurricane had swept on its northward course and the wind had dropped to almost a dead calm, that long-pent tide had come roaring in with breakers thirty to forty feet high, crashing over the very tops of the dunes themselves, ripping out great sections of beach and wreaking enormous havoc, especially up in the little town of Surf Crest to the north.

Captain Cy had told Mr. Burnett that he had been using the Coast Guard telephone to get news and had heard that part of the bridge connecting the island with the mainland had been swept away. Electric wires were down in all directions, and no communication could be had save through the Coast Guard telephones, which had miraculously escaped damage. He told him also that he would try to get word to Mrs. Kilroy on the mainland, through this channel, that her son was safe but that there was no hope of getting him home at present, as even most of the available boats had been sunk or swept away.

And so matters had had to rest. Mrs. Greene had that night made up a cot for Chips in the old parlor, and the first thing after breakfast he had volunteered to make himself useful by going out to chop away the obstructing tree. Ted had wanted to help him, but Monsieur had objected to such use of the boy's already damaged hands and had wafted him away to the station. Marty had found her strained ankle much improved that morning, and as she could hobble about on it without too much discomfort, she had insisted on getting up and giving what aid she could to the still very much upset Mrs. Greene.

Thus stood matters on that morning after the historic hurricane, as calm and sunny and charming a morning as could well be imagined. Marty glanced out at the boy in the yard, hacking away with his strong young arms, slicing off branch after branch of the fallen tree, making the chips fly in all directions.

"Poor Chips," she thought. "Back at the old job of chopping wood! I wonder what he's thinking about now? He did a grand job of rescuing Ted. If it hadn't been for him—" She shuddered and did not finish the thought but instead asked herself, "I wonder what he came over here for the other day, anyway?" As if sensing her unspoken thoughts, Chips suddenly straightened up, dropped his ax, wiped his forehead with his sleeve, and came up to the kitchen door.

"Say, Marty," he mumbled, "are you alone? I—I've got to have a talk with you for a few minutes. There isn't anyone else I can talk to. You—you've always understood me, sort of, better than most folks. I—I can tell this to you—and I can't to anyone else. Do you mind?"

"Why, of course not!" she said. "Nana's busy upstairs, and the rest are all out. We won't be disturbed for a while. Come right in."

It was a curious talk she had with Chips that morning—a very curious talk—and led to matters quite unforeseen by them both. He came in and seated himself uneasily, opening the interview by saying, "I suppose you know I was the one who stole that food, night before last, don't you?"

"We guessed it—even then," Marty admitted. "But you didn't really *steal* it, Chips. Nana found the money you left on the ice box to pay for it."

"Oh, *that*!" He shrugged. "That wouldn't have paid for half of it, but it was all I had. I had to have something ahead to eat—for a while. But how did you know it was me? I thought you'd probably think it was some tramp."

"We recognized your footprints, Chips," hesitated Marty. She knew he was rather sensitive about his slightly deformed foot but felt she must tell the truth. Then she added boldly, "Whatever did you come here for? To try to get—Thusy?"

The boy stared at her in patient astonishment. "*Me?*—take that bird?" he exclaimed. "What would I want *him* for?" His plainly truthful retort and his evident astonishment at the suggestion rather nonplussed Marty.

"Well, we knew your mother had always said that Thusy really belonged to you folks, and—and we thought maybe she'd gotten you to try to get him away from us somehow. I know it sounds— strange—but it was the only reason we could think of for you being around here—all night, and—getting into the house that way." Marty blushed hotly at having to make this explanation.

"Do you think I take any stock in that truck?" mumbled Chips unhappily. "If you do, you're miles away from the truth. I've always hated that nonsense of Ma's!" And Marty could not but believe him.

"Then—then why *did* you come over?" she demanded.

Grimly, Chips replied, "Because I was going to *run away*, that's why! I was so sick and tired of the way things are going at home that I couldn't stand it any longer. I wanted to quit school and go to work, but Ma wouldn't let me. Said I ought to finish high school—and anyway, she needed me around to help her at home. She doesn't—nothing of the sort! She's got money enough to hire someone to do all I do, but she won't spend it. Keeps me chopping wood and doing chores and running errands, and *you* know I never have any time to study decently. It's a wonder I've ever got as far as I have! So, I decided to chuck it all and—and just disappear!"

He considered the situation in gloomy silence till Marty broke it by inquiring, "But why then did you come over *here*, Chips? I—I should have thought it was a lot out of your way. Why not have started straight from across your side of the bay? Wouldn't it have been simpler?"

"I didn't think of that," he acknowledged, "but it wouldn't have worked. They'd have caught up with me too soon—and brought me back. I had a better scheme. We had the time off from school, and I could be around home, so I said I was going clamming, day before yesterday morning, after I got done with the work. I didn't say I was coming over here. I did dig some clams on the other side and then rowed across. But after I got out, I gave the boat a push and sent her out into the bay. I knew the tide would carry her down toward the inlet, and they'd probably find her adrift—and empty. And if I didn't show up myself, they'd probably think I'd fallen out—and drowned—or something like that. My plan was to hide around here till things blew over and then sneak out some dark night—and get to New York somehow, hitchhiking, and find a job there. I—"

"But, Chips," interrupted Marty in a shocked voice, "that would have been a terrible thing to do to your mother—to let her think you were—drowned! Don't you know that?"

"I—I guess it would have been—pretty raw," he acknowledged sheepishly. "I've been thinking it over since, and—and I realize that, too. But I'd planned to let her know—after I got a job and—and was sort of settled there. Then I thought maybe she'd give it up and let me stay there—if I was making some money and could send her some." It was a pathetic plan, and he must have been desperate to have thought of it—even Marty realized that.

"But jobs aren't easy to find these days," she remarked sagely, "and you might have starved before you got one."

"I know it now," he replied gloomily, "and it's all off anyway. The whole thing was a flop unless nobody knew I'd been over here. I spent that day looking around for a place I could hide, and I discovered that little shack where Ted and I were during the storm. It seemed like a good place, but the trouble was I hadn't anything to eat—and I was crazy hungry by nightfall. Then I thought of your place here, and when it was dark, I came here to scout around. I thought maybe I could get in by that pantry window while you were all talking in the kitchen, but the bench wobbled and threw me down. I ran off into the woods while you were scouting around trying to find out who it was. Then, after you'd all gone to bed, I did get in through the kitchen here and took the meat and bread.

"Someone scared me good and proper, yelling after me just as I got out. But as no one came out afterward, I spent the rest of the night in the barn. It was raining too hard to try to get down to the shack then. Early next morning, before it was light, I looked out and saw a light burning in the kitchen, and that scared me again. I figured Mrs. Greene was up and would probably come out to the barn looking for eggs—or something, and I just beat it out again as fast as I could—and over to the bay shore. I even forgot to take the food, I hustled away so fast! I went back to the little shack because it was raining so hard. But I got so hungry later on that I decided to sneak back and see if I couldn't get that grub when no one was about. I didn't think anyone would be out much on such a stormy day."

"And then you saw Ted and me coming along the shore," suggested Marty, smiling slightly, "and you hid behind Uncle Cy's little shed?"

"Yes," he agreed. "I saw you quite a way off, but I didn't think you were out looking for *me*! I didn't know that till Ted told me afterward. When Ted started to chase after me, I couldn't think what it was all about, and I kept ducking around, trying to keep out of sight. I ran around that bog and over toward the ocean and thought I'd lost him. But when I didn't see anything of him afterward, I began to get worried for fear he'd got into that bad marsh and might be in trouble. It kept teasing me till I had to come back and take a peek to see that he wasn't there. After that I was going to disappear into the shack. But he *was* there, and—well, you know the rest! I knew my own game was up when I went to pull him out—but, of course, I couldn't do anything else!"

"You were grand, Chips," said Marty softly. "I think it was finer than ever of you—now that I know the whole story!"

Chips brushed this praise aside brusquely. "That wasn't why I told it to you. I—I just wanted you to know I wasn't over here—stealing things and—and breaking into houses—for no reason. I wanted you to know how it was! And I've got to tell you another thing. I—I heard quite a good deal of what you were all talking about—that night in the kitchen when I was at the pantry window. I know I oughtn't to have been listening, but after I heard Mrs. Greene mention Grandfather's name, I—I just couldn't help it. I'd never heard that whole story straight—just Ma's side of it and a little my father once told me before he died. It was a whole lot different from what your grandmother told that night—and I guess her side is the truth! I'm sure as sure that if Sailor Jack ever had anything worthwhile to leave, that when he died, he left it to you folks. I wanted you to know that. And, just one thing more. I think I know something that would help you find—"

But he did not get a chance to finish his sentence, for, just at that moment, they heard Mr. Burnett, Ted, and Monsieur coming up the kitchen steps and knew that their moment for confidences was over.

"Tell you some other time," muttered Chips, and took himself back to his chopping.

XVI

THUSY TAKES THE SPOTLIGHT

It struck Marty that Mr. Burnett looked rather grave when he came in. He and the others were armed with large packages of supplies that he had promised to bring Mrs. Greene from town. When he had put them on the table, he announced:

"I bought up everything I could find in town, but supplies in some lines were limited because part of the bridge is down and regular foodstuffs can't get here till it's repaired—which may be several days. Things are even worse than we thought yesterday. However, I guess we won't starve. I was fortunate enough to catch the Coast Guard truck again, and they helped me bring all this down."

"Don't worry about starving!" laughed Marty. "Nana has a whole closet full of canned stuff that she puts up during the summer. We usually keep it for the winter, but it'll come in handy now."

"But that wasn't the worst of it," Mr. Burnett went on seriously. "While I was up in town, I heard rumors that the hurricane of yesterday was by no means over when it left us. In fact, we felt only the lighter part of it. Coming at us as it did, it struck us only a sort of glancing blow. When I saw it disappearing out to sea yesterday afternoon—the ugliest mass of black clouds imaginable—I certainly thought it had left our shores forever. But now it seems that it didn't. Instead of blowing northeastward to sea, it suddenly turned straight north and tore over Long Island and New England during the rest of yesterday afternoon and night. And as it struck head on in those localities, it has done the most appalling amount of damage and has caused also, they fear, a terrible loss of life. There are few details as yet available, for wires are down, roads are wrecked, and almost all forms of communication are out of order except by radio. So, you see, bad as conditions were here yesterday, we were fortunate compared to what went on farther north!"

They all looked very shocked at this news. And Mrs. Greene, who had come downstairs in time to hear most of it, remarked, "Well, it's the only time I ever heard of that the Jersey coast didn't get the worst of any big storm! We always bore the brunt—so Abner used to say!"

At this point, Ted strolled outside to talk to Chips, to whom he seemed to have taken quite a fancy since his rescue from the bog, and after he had gone, Mr. Burnett went on in a lower voice:

"While Ted is away, I want to tell you all something else which I'm anxious that he shouldn't hear. I understand that one of the localities hardest hit was Westhampton, on Long Island. They say that almost every house on the ocean side there is either partly or completely demolished. My only sister—Ted's aunt Edith—has one of those houses, a very delightful place, and she had urged us to spend this vacation of mine there. I did not accept the offer, for Ted used to spend much time there with his mother, and I feared the associations would be too painful for him, just at present. If we had gone there, it is very possible that we might not be alive this morning. But, in addition to that, I have the gravest fears for the safety of my sister. That she was there at this period, I know, for Ted had a letter from her only yesterday, written from that house. I tried to get some word from there when I was up in town this morning, but none could be got through. Conditions both there and here are too chaotic. So I shall just have to wait until they can be reestablished. If I could get away from here, I'd leave at once and try to get to the location. But, short of swimming to the mainland, there seems no way of getting off, and I shall have to wait a day or two till communications can be returned to something like normal. You'll all understand how anxious I am, but I do not want Ted to know anything about it, at present. He is very fond of his aunt, and he has had enough sorrow without—this!"

No one seemed to be able to utter a word of sympathy for his anxiety, but he understood their unspoken thoughts. Then he changed the subject abruptly.

"By the way, Mrs. Greene, there was a message I was asked to give you. I met Captain Cy on the way back here, and he told me his wife has been very much upset since yesterday's experience and is in bed with a nervous attack. He wanted to know if you and Marty could come over this afternoon and be with her for a while. I told him I'd see that you got there, for I think the water in the lane is disappearing enough so that I can take the car through it and land you at his house without difficulty."

"Dear, dear!" sighed Mrs. Greene. "Emmeline always was delicate and easily upset! And that storm was enough to scare her out of her wits. Yes, indeed! Marty and I will be glad to go, and you're very kind to offer to take us through that lane in the car."

And so it was arranged. They had an early dinner, and after it was over and the dishes disposed of, Mr. Burnett packed them into his car, and they started off. Ted and Monsieur were to go to the station and do a little practicing, as the pianos had been found to be in better shape than might have been expected. Mr. Burnett took his fishing rod, saying he would try to distract his mind by a few casts for striped bass. Only Chips elected to remain at the house and finish with his task of chopping away the tree. They could well understand that he would only feel ill at ease accompanying either of the two parties and would doubtless be much more comfortable left to his appointed task. They left him chopping sturdily at the main trunk, and it was two hours before they returned.

About an hour after she had arrived at the house of her uncle Cy, Marty became bored with sitting and listening to Mrs. Greene and her aunt Emmeline exchanging reminiscences of their experiences in the previous day's hurricane and hobbled over to the Coast Guard station. She had done all she could to help with the rather chaotic household affairs at her aunt's, and Gwen and the captain had gone up the beach to see the damage that had been wrought in the town. There being no further need for her to remain, and hearing sounds of the music she liked, she decided that it would be far more interesting over at the station.

She found Ted at one piano and Monsieur at the other, and a brilliant cascade of the most entrancing music was being executed—a composition with which she was not familiar.

"Now I know what the two pianos are for, at last!" she told herself as she sat and listened. "They're going to perform a duet!" But when they had come to a pause and she had ventured to ask what it was, Monsieur replied enthusiastically:

"Ah! Zis ees zee *Concerto in C Minor* by Beethoven. Eet ees, I sink, zee most entrancing one he ever wrote. But you cannot know how heavenly eet sound till you hear eet wis zee orchestra. Now we do zee second movement—zee *Largo*. Listen, Marty, to zee beautiful *arpeggios* zat Ted do so well. But me, I cannot give you zee exquisite orchestra accompaniment of zee bassoon and flute over zee *pizzicato* of zee strings!"

Marty did not quite understand it all, but she listened in a pleasant trance of delight as the music flowed from the two pianos, wondering the more at the musical gift of this slim boy who was to perform with an orchestra. Time slipped by as she listened, and all too soon Mr. Burnett came back carrying two "stripers," and suggested that they return to the house. And, having picked up Mrs. Greene, they sloshed back through the lane, which still resembled a young river, the water up to the hubs of the car.

Out at the rear of the house, they saw no sign of Chips, though the tree still lay not completely demolished. A sudden fear darted through Marty's mind that he might have run off again while they had left him alone, but she did not mention it. After all, she considered, he could not get very far under the circumstances. She was utterly unprepared for the curious sight they beheld on entering the kitchen. For there Chips was sitting at the table, his fists clenched on it, his face pale with some emotion they could not fathom, and his black eyes wide and frightened.

"Why, Chips!" cried Marty. "What in the world is the matter?"

The boy stared at them all despairingly and swallowed hard before answering, "It's—it's Thusy! He—he's *gone!*"

They gasped in dismay and for the first time noticed that the macaw's perch was empty.

"Gone?—Gone *where?*" demanded Mrs. Greene, who could not believe her eyes.

"I wish I knew!" groaned the miserable Chips.

"But, how did he get away?" cried Marty. "He—he *couldn't* get loose from that chain—by himself!"

"It's all my fault!" blurted Chips. "I might as well tell you that to start with. I—I came in here for a drink of water a while ago—and—and while I was here, Thusy said something that made me think maybe I could try an experiment. So—so I loosened the fastening on his chain. But first, I went all through the house to—to see that there was no place where he could get out." Poor Chips was gulping with embarrassment and despair between almost every two words, but he struggled on:

"I—just sat here and watched him. He didn't fly off right away but—but at last he found he was free, and—and all of a sudden—he spread his wings and flew out into the hall. I still sat right here because I didn't want to scare him—so I don't know just where he went from there. I was sure I could find him when I hunted him up. By and by, I got up to look for him. He—he wasn't anywhere on this floor—so I went upstairs. I looked in every room—but he wasn't in any of them. I—I even went up to the tower—but he wasn't there either. Then I got scared! I ran all over the place again. I looked under all the furniture, everywhere I could think—but he seemed to be gone. I—I don't know *where* he could have got out. I—I'm sorrier than I can tell you—"

He almost broke down at this point, and Mr. Burnett asked hastily, "But why did you do it, Chips? Why did you let him loose? What did he say that made you think of it?"

The boy pulled himself together and half sobbed, "He—he said a strange thing. While I was getting my drink of water and not noticing him at all, he said, sort of like he was talking to himself, 'Hide it, Jack!—Hide it, Jack!' And then he said afterward, 'I'll never tell!' It—it made me think of something I heard my father tell once when he was talking about this business of Sailor Jack and—and my grandfather. Seems my grandfather had once come over here to see Sailor Jack and was told he was out in the barn. Before he went into the barn, he heard Sailor Jack talking in there, and he stopped and listened. Seems Sailor Jack was either talking to himself or to the parrot. He was saying, 'I'm going to hide it, Thusy, where no one else can find it but you and me—do you hear? Hide it!' And the parrot began to say, 'Hide it!—Hide it!' over and over. And Sailor Jack laughed and then began to teach him to say, 'I'll never tell!' Grandfather didn't go into the barn that day because he didn't want Sailor Jack to know he had been listening. But he always declared that the parrot knew where Sailor Jack had hidden his money, so my father said."

They were all startled at this intriguing explanation of the singular phrase Thusy sometimes used. But Chips went on:

"So, when I heard Thusy say that this afternoon, it suddenly made me think that if I could let him loose for a while, he might go to where it was hidden, and then I could surprise you all by showing you where it was—when you got back. I—I didn't want it for myself. You must believe me! Though perhaps you think it looks that way. I didn't come over here for that. Marty knows. I told her the real reason this morning."

"Indeed you did, Chips!" cried Marty, hotly championing him. "And if you don't mind, I'm going to tell the folks right now what you told me." Chips nodded in assent, and Marty quickly recounted to them the story Chips had told her that morning. Then she went on bravely, "So, you see, Chips' being here didn't have a thing to do with anything concerning Thusy. He—he told me he knew something that might help us, but he didn't get a chance to finish before you all came in. And now I know this was it!"

It was Mr. Burnett who made the first response to the pathetic story of the boy's attempted escape from his unpleasing life.

"I didn't need to hear this, Chips," he said, "to believe that your intentions were of the best and most straightforward. No boy who had done what you did yesterday would be capable of a dishonest action!"

A slow flush mounted into the boy's face, and he stammered, "Thank you, sir!"

But Mr. Burnett hurried on, "Now, about this disappearance of Thusy! It doesn't seem possible that he could have got out of the house. He *must* have some hidey-hole we don't know about. So I suggest that we go over the place again and make a thorough search of every room. He certainly isn't in the kitchen, but it's just possible that when Chips was hunting in one spot, the bird may have flown to another and then back again and has kept eluding him in that way. It could be done with only *one* person doing the hunting. Now there are six of us, and we can deploy all through the house so that he can't fly back and forth without being seen by *someone*!"

They entered into the hunt with enthusiasm. The three older people deployed over the lower floor, while Marty, Ted, and Chips undertook the search in the upper rooms and even the little tower. No nook, corner, or crack escaped their attention, and when they had reassembled in the kitchen, the sum and substance of their whole effort was only one little blue feather that Ted had picked up at the foot of the steep stairs leading to the tower or cupola.

Glumly they compared notes and agreed that Thusy could not have disappeared more successfully.

"But, I beg of you not to worry, Mrs. Greene," said Mr. Burnett. "I remember that Marty told me Thusy did this very same thing once before, when you were both away, and came back safely, though you could never find out where he'd been or how he got out and back. And even if he has got out, I'm very certain Thusy is too old a bird, and too used to being right here, to wander away far. I think he'll come back—and the thing will be to find out how he does it."

The words had scarcely left his mouth when, with a great whirring and flapping of wings, Thusy soared into the kitchen from the hall and settled on his perch. Sheer amazement kept them silent till Mrs. Greene finally struggled to her feet, clasped the chain on his leg, and demanded, "Thusy, where in the world *have* you been?"

Thusy scratched his head with one claw and emitted a sound strangely like a wicked chuckle. After which he condescended to squawk:

"Go fly a kite!"

XVII

CHIPS SOLVED THE RIDDLE

THEY ALL COLLAPSED IN HELPLESS laughter at the impudence of the retort. And when they had recovered, Mr. Burnett eagerly made a suggestion.

"I have an idea," he declared. "And, if it would be agreeable to you, Mrs. Greene, I'd very much like to give it a try. This seems to be as good a time as we could get for it. I'm convinced that Thusy hasn't been in the house all this time. If you notice, his feathers are rather rumpled, and there's a piece of old straw sticking in his tail. He certainly wouldn't have got that indoors, I think. Now, if my plan works, we may be able to discover where he gets out and also where he goes, when and if he does. Would you be willing for us to let him loose again, Mrs. Greene?"

"I don't see what harm it can do," agreed that lady. "He comes back every time, and I'm pretty sure he's too old and not used to flying anymore to go far."

"Very well, then," went on Mr. Burnett. "Now, here's my plan. We'll all, except you, Mrs. Greene, go outside the house and post ourselves around it, on every side, far enough away so that we can, between us, see every corner and side of it. We'll keep hidden and out of sight, as much as possible, so that the sight of us won't distract him when he gets outdoors. Then, when we're all posted, I'll whistle a signal, and then will you just unfasten his chain and let him do whatever he likes? I think, in that way, we may be able to trace where this wily old bird takes himself!"

The plan was greeted with enthusiasm by them all, and while Mrs. Greene waited in the kitchen, the rest all trouped out, each to be tucked away in some concealed spot by Mr. Burnett, where a clear view of the house could be had.

"Now, mind," he warned them, "if you see him coming out anywhere, don't make a sound that would frighten him, but watch in what direction he flies off. And then, as soon as you can, without startling him, get to me as quickly as possible. I'll be over among those bushes near the barn door." He hurried to his own post, and presently Mrs. Greene heard his shrill whistle and knew that the time for the great experiment had come.

As she approached Thusy, the macaw winked at her with one solemn eye and complained: "Thusy very—very hungry!"

"Never mind—you ain't to get fed just now!" she announced, at the same time loosening and dropping the chain from his leg. At first, he seemed rather surprised—as well he might be!—and lifted his free leg and surveyed it curiously. Then, suddenly, as if realizing anew his strange freedom, he spread his wings and sailed out of the room. Mrs. Greene wanted desperately to follow and see where he went, but she had been warned not to do that, lest she upset the plan. So she seated herself in her rocker and waited in trembling suspense for what seemed an interminable period.

"Probably he won't do it again!" she told herself. "He's that perverse!"

But even as she thought it, Ted rushed in, announcing, "We saw him! We all did, right at the same time! He came out of somewhere in the tower and flew straight to the barn. He got in there by that little broken window in the harness room. They're all out there now, but he's disappeared somewhere in the barn. We're going to hunt for him. Won't you come out and help us?" Ted was so excited that his face was scarlet, and his big blue eyes looked as if they would pop right out of his head.

Wonderingly, Mrs. Greene assented, and they both hurried to the barn. Mr. Burnett let them in and carefully closed the harness room door. To Ted's eager questioning, he said, "No, we haven't found where he is yet. I've stuffed up that broken window with rags, so he can't get out again that way, and we're going to give this place a thorough combing. I feel certain now that it must have been somewhere in here that Sailor Jack hid his treasure, since it has never been found in the house. And, from what Chips has told us, there's a bare chance that Thusy may know the spot and has gone to it. But it's up to us to locate it—or at least find the whereabouts of Thusy. You don't know of any possible hiding places here, do you, Mrs. Greene?"

"Never heard of one—nor saw it either." She shook her head. "And I know this barn like it was my own bedroom!"

"Well, then, we'll just have to go over the whole place," he announced. "Monsieur, will you be so good as to stand out in the middle of the barn proper and keep looking about to see that Thusy doesn't fly out from anywhere while we're busy elsewhere? We'll give this room a thorough going over first and then try the larger space outside."

And so the great parrot and treasure hunt began! The harness room was soon disposed of. It was a comparatively small space and yielded nothing save the remains of the lamb and loaf of bread that Chips had confiscated on that evening, which now seemed so long ago. They were very moldy and nibbled by mice. Without further ado, they all moved out into the main barn and scattered about, examining every nook and cranny with no success whatsoever. There remained only the hayloft above, reached by the ladder up which Mrs. Greene and Monsieur refused to climb, leaving that part of the task to the younger and sprier members of the party.

The hayloft was the space above the stalls and the harness

room. At a casual glance, it contained nothing whatever except a scattering of ancient and moldy hay, most of it in the pile Chips had fashioned into a bed, covered by the old blanket the night he slept there. There were also two chutes for tossing down hay into the stalls below. There was apparently nothing else—and no visible sign of Thusy. Mr. Burnett examined the floor carefully for any signs of a loose board, as he had in the harness room and the lower part of the barn, and was nearly finished with his scrutiny when suddenly Chips pounced on something in a corner, among the shreds of hay, and held it up in triumph.

It was two small yellow feathers from the breast of Thusy's burnished crop—there could be no mistaking them!

"Ha!" cried Mr. Burnett. "*Now* we have a lead! Where in the world can that old fellow be? He's certainly been somewhere near here."

"Look up there—over your head!" shouted Ted. "What's that line of old boxes up near the roof?"

"Those are old pigeon boxes," called up Mrs. Greene from below. "Sailor Jack built those, but they haven't been used for years and years. He had a fancy for keeping pigeons once and built those boxes to hold their nests—way up near the roof because they don't like to nest near the ground."

"Well, we've got the answer, I think!" called back Mr. Burnett. "But they're above my head. Help me haul up that ladder, Chips, and we'll investigate." The ladder was soon pulled up and placed beside the box under which Thusy's feathers had been found, and Mr. Burnett climbed it. But before he had reached where he could peer into the box, there was a familiar whirring and flapping of wings as Thusy scrambled out of the box and flew squawking about the barn, lighting at last on a beam, where he screeched indignantly, "Go fly a kite!" over and over, answering the delighted yells that burst from all the searchers—even from Mrs. Greene!

"Now look in the box!" cried Ted, hopping up and down in excitement and suspense. They all watched breathlessly while Mr.

Burnett poked his head over the top of the box to peer in, then groped about in it with one hand. Presently, he called down to them in a disgusted voice:

"There's absolutely nothing in here except some old hay and bits of shells—pigeon eggshells, I guess!" There was a chorus of disappointed groans.

"Why not look in the other boxes?" suggested Marty. "Maybe Thusy made a mistake." It was a sensible suggestion, and moving the ladder along, Mr. Burnett made a search of every one of the half dozen—with no better success.

Clambering down the ladder, he remarked, "I guess we're all off the track, as far as that black box is concerned. Thusy's certainly led us on a nice wild-goose chase! If there's any black box still in existence, it doesn't seem to be here."

A depressed silence fell on them all—the more depressed because of the hopes that had been falsely raised. Thusy, meanwhile, had quieted down and was silent, too, as he sat surveying them from his perch on the beam with what seemed a rather sarcastic interest.

"Well, I suppose we might as well get back to the house," Mr. Burnett at last remarked. "No use trying to catch Thusy. He'll no doubt follow in his own good time."

"Wait just a minute!" begged Chips, who had been quietly surveying, by the light of a flashlight, the box from which Thusy had flown. "I—I have an idea. It may not be any good, but it's worth a try!" He took the ladder from below the farthest box where Mr. Burnett had left it and placed it once more under the box in the corner where Thusy had emerged. Mounting it, he took a large penknife from his pocket, opened it, and seemed to be measuring the depth of the box both on the outside and within. Nodding his head in a satisfied way, he called down:

"I think we've got something here! This box seems to be nearly three inches deeper on the outside than it is inside. Maybe it has a false bottom!"

Immediately the watchers came to life again and shouted to him to try it and see. He scooped out the cluttering hay and debris, then ran his knife around the inside flooring of the box. There was a breathless moment of suspense while Chips worked away, saying not a word. Then they saw him use the other hand, then tug with them both. And, in another instant, he held something up in the air and shouted:

"*Here's your black box!*"

❦

They were all back in the kitchen, sitting around the table, with the black box reposing in the center of it. It was not a very imposing black box and not very large—some twelve inches long, four inches wide, and not more than two in height. It was heavy, with a metal foundation and a black enamel covering, some of which had been chipped off in the course of the years. It was fastened with a hasp and a little padlock to which there was no key. This much could be seen at a casual glance, and they were all now wondering what could be done about opening it. Ted, who was very impatient, was all for breaking it open with some tool, and Mr. Burnett was inclined to agree that there seemed no other method.

But Mrs. Greene suddenly exclaimed, "Wait a minute! Seems a shame to break that little padlock if we don't have to. I remember, years ago, when we packed away the few things Sailor Jack left after he died, that there was a little key among the things in his bureau drawer. I never knew what it was for—seemed too small for most things, and I never saw anything it fitted. I'll go upstairs and hunt it up right now in the box where we put his belongings."

While she was gone, Marty said, "That was awfully smart of you, Chips, to think of that pigeon box having a false bottom! Do tell us how you figured it out."

"Oh, it wasn't very hard," he replied, as usual blushing furiously. "It was really quite simple. First, I noticed that that box was quite a bit larger than the five others, but the thing that got me thinking was when I turned Mr. Burnett's flashlight on it and noticed that there was a row of nail points along the side of it about three inches from the bottom. I couldn't quite figure what those nails were for, just in a plain box with the side all one solid piece of wood. So I thought we'd better find out before we left it. The nails were to fasten in a little ledge of wood that supported the false bottom. The other side had one just like it. The false bottom was a very thin piece of wood. It didn't take up much space. And it was just fastened down to the ledges with two nails on each side. I didn't have any trouble prying it up. That's all there was to it!"

"You're a noticing and resourceful lad, Chips," said Mr. Burnett briefly but appreciatively. And at that moment, Mrs. Greene reappeared with a small key in her hand.

The most intense moment of their mystery had come! No one except Mrs. Greene had noticed that the afternoon had waned and that the kitchen, bereft of sunlight, was growing dark. She handed the key to Mr. Burnett and lighted the big oil lamp, setting it in the middle of the table.

"You must open this box yourself, Mrs. Greene," he said, when she had resumed her seat. But she waved that aside.

"My hand shakes too much," she quavered nervously. "You'd better do it, if you'll be so kind."

"Very well, if you wish it!" he answered, fitting the key into the little padlock. But the lock was rusty, and he asked for a drop of oil to limber it up. When Marty had brought him a cupful from their supply, he dropped one drop in and continued to work the key gently back and forth, much to Ted's distress, who cried:

"Oh, *do* hurry up, Dad! This suspense is just too *awful*!"

Marty couldn't help but giggle at that. But at last Mr. Burnett gave a sigh of satisfaction. The key had begun to turn, and in another moment, the padlock opened and fell on the table.

"Now, Mrs. Greene," he said, handing her the box, "this is strictly your affair, and you must be the first to see its contents."

With hands that trembled as with palsy, she took the box and threw back the lid while all crowded about her to get a peep. There was nothing on the top but a layer of jeweler's cotton, yellowed with age. This she removed, and underneath appeared a letter in a sealed envelope, addressed to her husband and herself in fine, rather "copperplate" writing, the ink now turned to a light brown. Upon removing this, there was revealed a chamois leather bag, drawn together at the top with a brown silken cord. Beneath that was another layer of cotton, and that was all the box contained.

"What had I best do first?" she asked Mr. Burnett. "Open the bag—or read the letter?"

"I should advise reading the letter," he suggested. And at this pronouncement, there was another groan from Ted.

Mrs. Greene handed the letter to Marty and said, "You'll have to read it, child! My eyesight ain't what it was, and this writing's too fine and faded." And, with the greatest thrill she had yet known, Marty casually tore open the sealed envelope, which contained several closely written sheets of notepaper, smoothed them out, and began:

> "June 11, 1912
>
> "Captain and Mrs. Greene:
>
> "You have both always been very kind to me, and have given me a home, for which the sum I paid you seemed quite inadequate. It has been more than a home. It has been a refuge to me from the storms and stresses of this world—a haven of peace such as I had not dreamed of ever possessing. I feel that I owe you a great debt of gratitude.
>
> "I am no longer young, and of late my heart has been acting strangely—so strangely that I am certain now that I have a trouble there that may some day carry me off. Therefore I am writing this letter to you, explaining some matters which I would like you to understand, but which I cannot bring myself to talk about while I am yet here. I shall place it in this black box, which I intend

to conceal in a secure hiding place. And I shall leave a short note in my bureau drawer, telling you how to find that hiding place."

"He never did!" interrupted Mrs. Greene, at this point. "I went all through his bureau—after he was gone—but there wasn't any note. That's strange!"

"I imagine he put off writing it—from month to month," commented Mr. Burnett. "During his first severe illness, he tried to tell you of its location but didn't quite succeed. Then, when he recovered, he probably thought he'd have another one sometime, of a similar character, in which he'd have a chance to speak of it instead of writing the note. No doubt he never realized he'd go so quickly."

"That must have been it," she sighed. "Go on with it, Marty!" And Marty continued reading:

"I feel that I should tell you I am no common sailor, as I pretended to be when I first came to you. I have acted as a sailor before the mast at times, for a number of years, but I was not born to that calling. Neither was I forced by circumstances to be so. But I have always loved the sea, and occasionally I chose to travel from land to land by way of enlisting as an able seaman.

"It is only right that you should know a little of my background and history, so I must tell you that I was born a member of the French nobility. I shall not reveal my real name or title, however. That secret must go with me to the end. The name you know me by has been assumed since I fled Paris in 1879. It is sufficient, and it is much the best that my true name should remain unknown forever.

"My family had been of the French nobility since before the time of the French Revolution. It was an ancient and very wealthy family. Considerable of this wealth was concealed after the overthrow of King Louis XVI, and what remained of it had descended to me. Our family never favored the Republic of France, and our one dominating thought was to restore the Bourbon monarchy to its throne, at some time when the occasion seemed ripe. We were not alone in this, as many others of our station in life possessed the same thoughts and plans. It was in such an attempt that I met the downfall which drove me, an exile and a refugee, from my native land.

"In a certain secret plot to overthrow the Republic and restore the monarchy, a traitor in our midst revealed the plot to the authorities. We, the ringleaders, of whom I was one, were suddenly rounded up at a secret meeting and were thrown into prison. Miraculously, I escaped, through the aid of a relative on the outside. I do not wish to go further into the history of this affair—and it is not necessary.

"This relative, who has long since passed to his reward, smuggled me on board an outgoing steamer as a common sailor before the mast, first having placed in my hands all that remained of my share of the family fortune, in the way of some valuable jewelry and gold. He warned me that it would be well never to try to set foot in the land of France again. And I never have.

"Since then I have wandered about the world, visiting strange countries, living simply, traveling often as a common sailor when it was necessary to cross the ocean, economizing what was left me of that fortune against the time when it might be necessary in my old age. The gold has long since been spent, and, when occasion required, I have sold one of the jewels. If I liked a strange country, I stayed there till boredom or necessity drove me on to another. It was in this fashion that I came upon Methuselah a few years ago, in one of the French colonies of South America. I saw him for sale in the marketplace of the town. He spoke certain French phrases remarkably well, and it cheered me to hear them. I felt I must have him, though the price the native asked for him was little less than robbery. So he became mine and has been with me ever since. To him, at least, I can talk as I would to no one else. It seems, at times, as if he had almost human intelligence.

"So, dear friends, this is my story—as much of it as I can ever tell you. I feel that I shall never live to see the monarchy restored to France, though it is still my dearest wish. Perhaps, someday, there may be a great war and present governments may totter. Then the French throne may be restored. Who knows!"

"By the way, Mrs. Greene," interrupted Mr. Burnett once more, "just when did Sailor Jack die? I'm curious to know."

"It was in—let's see—1914," she replied. "Early in August. I don't just remember the exact date."

"Just as I thought!" he exclaimed. "He was looking for some great, upheaving war—and there it was—the World War—just begun in full ferocity in Belgium! He was reading a newspaper, I think you said, and probably the shock of realizing that here was just the situation for which he had been waiting was too much for his weakened heart. Perhaps it's just as well he did not live to see it turn out quite differently from what he had hoped! But now, Marty, read on."

"There's only one more paragraph," said Marty. "Here it is:

"After I am gone, I wish you to have what remains in the black box. As I have said before, it is all too inadequate to repay your great kindness to me, but it is what I have left in the world, and I have no kith or kin to claim it. Keep Methuselah with you always. He is very dear to me, and I know you will care for him tenderly. Again, I thank you both and wish you well.

"Jacques Montagne"

There was a moment's silence in the lamplit room—a silence dedicated to the memory of the departed "Sailor Jack" and his curious and eventful history. No one noticed that outside twilight was falling, that only remnants of a fading sunset remained in the west—and that Thusy's perch was still empty. Suddenly the silence was broken by a great whir and flapping of wings, and the wandering Thusy sailed in from the hall and settled on his perch near the table. He appeared to eye the black box with considerable interest, and then, as if some memory had been stirred in him, he rose on his perch, flapped his wings, and screeched:

"*Vive le roi!*"

"Couldn't have been more appropriate if he had been human!" laughed Mr. Burnett, breaking the tension. "Perhaps Sailor Jack was right! That was a revealing and pathetic document. And now, Mrs. Greene, don't you want to examine the contents of that bag?"

"Poor old Jack!" sighed Mrs. Greene, whose eyes had filled with tears at the end of the letter's reading. "He certainly had a hard life. But he was a real gentleman—we always knew he was!" She took up the little chamois bag and, with fingers that trembled, emptied its contents out on the table.

Before their astonished eyes lay a small heap of gems, some set in now blackly tarnished gold settings, some not set at all. Diamonds and emeralds winked and sparkled in the lamplight and, even to an unpracticed eye, revealed themselves of undoubted beauty and value. The breathtaking spectacle robbed them of any adequate comment, except enthusiastic "Ohs!" and "Ahs!" Mr. Burnett took them up one by one, to examine them with careful scrutiny, especially those mounted in the gold settings—mostly rings.

"I was hoping to find some emblem or family crest on some of these," he commented, "that might give us a clue to Sailor Jack's noble family, but I see there are none. I rather fancy that those unset gems may have once been mounted with some such marking, and he had been careful to remove these, lest his ancestry be discovered. These are certainly a valuable collection. I congratulate you, my dear lady!"

"But—but what am I going to do with them?" quavered Mrs. Greene in hopeless bewilderment. "Marty or I wouldn't ever want to wear such grand things as these! They ain't suitable—they look like they ought to be in a museum!"

"You can always sell them," said Mr. Burnett, "and that is what I advise you to do. If you like, I can have a first-class, reliable jeweler come down from the city and appraise them for you and give you their honest value. They ought to be worth a considerable sum—in fact, I should say, offhand, a good number of thousand dollars!"

"If you'll do that," gulped Mrs. Greene, "I—I—" But words had failed her completely. And, too proud to break down before the others, she snatched off her glasses, which were misted with tears, and hurried out of the room, while Mr. Burnett thoughtfully gathered up the gems and returned them to the leather bag.

Suddenly there was a knock at the kitchen door, and Captain Cy poked in his head a moment to announce, "I just hurried over to bring you a bit of good news, Mr. Burnett. Got it over the Coast Guard telephone just now. Seems your sister that you was worrying about has been trying to get in touch with you all afternoon. She finally got a radiogram to the radio station across the bay, and they telephoned it to the Coast Guard station at South Inlet. Seems she *wasn't* out on Long Island last night in the hurricane. She'd come in to New York the day before to do some shopping and stayed over at her house in the city. Says she guesses her house at Westhampton's swept away, but she's all right. Wants to know how you and Ted are and what the storm did to you. Sorry I can't stay, but Emmeline's still pretty sick, and I promised I'd come right back. So long!"

The Captain was gone before he could even be thanked. And with a fervent, "Thank the Lord!" Mr. Burnett turned to explain the situation to the wondering Ted, who could now be told what had been agonizing his father all that afternoon.

It was a lighthearted, almost unbelievably happy party that gathered about the supper table later that evening. The striped bass, caught by Mr. Burnett that afternoon, were sizzling deliciously on a platter, and even Thusy had been treated to one of his favorite bananas, which he was now eating with gratified chuckles and clucks. It was Ted who suddenly, between two mouthfuls, voiced a question that no one as yet had thought to ask.

"What *I* want to know," he inquired, "is how in the world Thusy got out of this house! We saw him come from somewhere around the tower, but there can't be any opening there."

Mrs. Greene chuckled. "That's just where you are mistaken," she remarked. "Soon as I heard he'd come from the tower, I knew exactly what happened. Funny that I'd forgot all about it till then! You see, those tower windows are fixed solid in. They don't open. Abner built 'em that way because they are sort of curved glass—came from the pilothouse of an old steamer—and he thought if they opened, they might get banging around and broken sometime. He was mighty proud of 'em, and they couldn't be replaced. But I've always liked to sit up there at times. And it's a small place, and in the warm weather, it'd get terrible hot and breathless. So Abner put in some ventilating spaces to cool it off. They're about five inches wide and run under the edges of the roof on the four sides. You can't see 'em unless you know they're there. In the winter they can be closed up with chocks of wood that fit in 'em. Sailor Jack used to like to sit up there sometimes, with Thusy, and I shouldn't wonder if he taught Thusy to get through 'em and fly out to the barn. He used to let him loose once in a while. That's all there is to it!"

"Oh!" cried Marty, clapping her hand to her forehead. "*I* knew that those ventilators were there all the time, too—and never thought of it. How absolutely *silly* of me!"

So vehemently did she pronounce it that the word caught the attention of the macaw. Dropping his banana, he began to screech, "Silly!—silly!—silly!—silly!" till Mrs. Greene exclaimed impatiently, "Oh, hush, Ihusy, or I'll put you in your cage!" Then, as if talking to herself, she murmured in a meditative undertone:

"The first thing I get will be that oil-burning heater!"

XVIII

ONE NOVEMBER NIGHT

On the stage of a certain concert hall in New York, a slim young boy sat at a grand piano. The stage was lighted, but the rest of the hall was darkened. The audience could not be seen by the boy who was drawing such remarkable strains of melody from the piano keys.

When the concert had begun, he had been very nervous, as he had feared he would be. But confidence had in some measure returned to him as he rendered the selections that were to precede his performance with the orchestra. There had been clamorous applause after each selection from that dark space, which contained the audience whose faces he could not see. He had risen and bowed repeatedly as these waves of applause greeted him, but he was not thinking of the audience.

He was not even thinking of his father and his aunt, who, he knew, were seated listening in the nearest box, probably more nervous than he was himself. He was not thinking of Monsieur, hovering anxiously behind the stage, watching his every note.

He was thinking only of Marty and Chips and Mrs. Greene in that far-off, warm old kitchen he had come to like so well—

thinking of them and knowing that they were listening to him over the big battery-set radio. The radio had been his and his father's parting gift to Marty when they had left two weeks before. For, even then, they had known that this concert was to be broadcast over one of the big national networks.

He was thinking of Heron Shoals and his long, quiet weeks of practice in the old Coast Guard station. This had been Marty's advice to him, shortly before he left, when he had confessed to her that he was terribly nervous about playing in public.

"I can do perfectly well here," he had admitted, "where I don't think at all about who's listening. The music comes from my fingers just naturally. But as soon as there are strangers listening, it seems to confuse me. Then I have to think of the notes I'm playing and think of the strangers, and I don't do well at all. That's why I'm nervous about the concert."

"Well, do you know what I think you ought to do?" Marty had advised. "Just make yourself believe you're down here—right in the station—that night of the concert. Forget all about those people and pretend you're here alone—with just Monsieur. Make yourself hear the sound of the waves and the gulls calling, and see the old mess room, just as it is now. I believe you'd forget all about the concert hall—and that audience. Couldn't you try that?" And he had promised to try.

"I'm sure I can do that with the first solos I'm to play," he had told her. "But when I come to the concerto with the orchestra, I have to concentrate my whole mind on what I'm doing. It's very difficult and very hard work. The only part I dread in that is the introduction, where the orchestra plays alone, and I just sit and do nothing till it's time to begin. I'll think about you all here till it's nearly time for me to start."

Now he was rendering the Chopin A-flat Major Polonaise. That always made him think of his first Sunday afternoon at Heron Shoals, how he and Marty had sat on the dunes listening to Monsieur in the station beautifully rendering this self-same number. And how the unwelcome Kilroys had come in sight—the shambling, sullen Chips, who was later to play such a startling role in his own life. And, as he rolled out the resounding and ascending chords that always reminded him of breakers crashing higher and higher on the beach, he thought of the recent and remarkable change in Chips—how the shambling and the sullenness were gone, banished by the plans his father had made for the boy—of the long and serious talk his father had had with Mrs. Kilroy at the time that hurricane conditions had at last been overcome and his father had driven Chips back to his home. In that conversation, his father had made her promise to allow her son to finish his high school course without interference, after which Chips was to be put into training in New York, under his father's own guidance, to fit him for the kind of work he found most congenial. In some unknown manner, his father had been able to prevail with the difficult Mrs. Kilroy, and Chips had been a changed lad ever since!

Suddenly there was tremendous applause. The boy realized that he had come to the end of the polonaise. He rose and bowed again and again and was finally allowed to retire from the stage, to be hugged and kissed on both cheeks by the exultant Monsieur! The first part of the concert had come to an end. He was to have a few minutes of well-earned rest before he returned to perform the concerto with the orchestra, which was even now filing out to take its place on the stage.

The dim old kitchen at Heron Shoals was filled with the sound of wild applause that rose and fell like the waves of the sea. The sounds came from an elaborate radio set, across the room from the range. Marty leaned forward with an ecstatic sigh and half whispered, "Wasn't he *wonderful?*"

Mrs. Greene and Chips, no less enthusiastic but lacking in the power of expression, nodded vigorously to indicate their agreement.

The kitchen was in no way changed from what it had been

several weeks ago (save for the radio), though Mrs. Greene now possessed a fat and comfortable bank account resulting from the sale of Sailor Jack's jewels. She had not yet decided how she would like to spend some of it on improvements in the uncomfortable old house, but she had privately made up her mind to reserve most of it for Marty's future education and well-being. The one thing that had been ordered was her longed-for oil heater, but that had not yet arrived.

It seemed as if the applause would never die down. Thusy, who liked and listened quietly to radio music, did not, however, care for racket and began to squawk, "Just a minute!" and "Don't get excited!" till Marty hushed him up by presenting a cracker.

Chips' one contribution to the comment was, "The clever little tyke!" Chips himself did not particularly care for or understand classical music, but he fully appreciated the talent that could elicit such an enthusiastic response. In the comparative quiet that ensued, while they could hear the orchestra tuning up and the announcer sketching a history of the concerto about to be performed, Marty remarked:

"This part is what Ted was most nervous about. But he promised me he wouldn't think a thing about the audience tonight, but only about us here and how he used to practice it at the station, to the sound of the ocean and the gulls. I wonder if he'll keep to that promise!"

Suddenly the announcer stopped talking. There was a long roll of orchestral instruments introducing the theme of the concerto—a theme now very familiar to Marty through hearing Monsieur play it so many times. It sounded somewhat different now, with the orchestral instruments. Then, after several moments, with three ascending, liquid runs, the piano came in, merging presently into the general theme but dominating it in clear, firm notes.

The old kitchen was flooded with glorious melody. Even Chips sat entranced, marveling that the young lad he had pulled from a dangerous quagmire on that day of the hurricane could possibly be producing part of this heavenly concord of sound. Marveling, too, at what that rescue had meant to his own personal fortunes. Life, he considered, was certainly a strange affair!

No one said a word during that wonderful half hour except once, when Marty was heard to murmur:

"Now I know what Monsieur meant about the piano *arpeggios* against the theme for the bassoon and flute, and the *pizzicato* accompaniment of the strings!" The others knew nothing of what she was talking about and let it go without comment.

At last, with a sweeping *cadenza*—which Marty remembered Ted as faithfully practicing over and over, hour after hour—the concerto drew to its gay and brilliant close. Ted's execution of his difficult part had been faultless. The audience seemed to have gone wild, judging from the thunderous applause that came over the radio.

In the dim kitchen, it beat upon the very walls and again aroused Thusy to a frenzied squawking. But after a while, it died away, and they heard someone asking Ted if he would speak to the audience. Evidently, too, a microphone had been brought close to him. Out of the nowhere that is radio, they heard his dear and familiar voice almost stammering:

"Thank you—everybody! Thank you! Thank you!" They thought then that it was all over, but there was one more thrill still to come. For, closer and more intimately, they heard Ted's voice speaking again:

"Goodnight, Marty—and Chips!"

And Marty knew that he had kept his promise!

THE END

VOCABULARY

AGOG – filled with intense interest and excitement
BREECHES BUOY – a rope-rigged rescue device, somewhat like a zip line, used for transferring and retrieving people from one place to another during emergency situations
CANNILY – carefully; with thoughtfulness; shrewdly
CHAMOIS – soft leather made from sheep or lamb skin
HASP – a metal plate used for fastening shut a lid or door, hinged, with a slot that fits over a metal loop that is then secured by a metal pin or padlock
LOQUACITY – talkativeness
MÉNAGE – household
NONPLUSSED – (verb) to surprise someone so much that they are unsure how to respond
OVERFALL – where ocean water is turbulent as it flows over submerged shoals or ridges or is whipped by wind
PELLUCIDLY – admitting the most light possible without distortion or diffusion
REMONSTRATE – to forcefully argue against
SINGULAR – strange, unusual, not ordinary
SURF CASTING – a technique for fishing where the bait is cast into the sea where the waves break onto the beach
TENTER – a framed device for stretching cloth between two clips or hooks
TENTERHOOKS – a sharp, hooked nail used for attaching cloth to a tenter
VOCIFEROUSLY – with a vehement or insistent outcry